PASSPORT TO A HAPPY DEATH

PASSPORT TO A HAPPY DEATH

✦

A CHRISTIAN HANDBOOK ON LIVING AND DYING

Diana Ingram

iUniverse, Inc.
New York Lincoln Shanghai

PASSPORT TO A HAPPY DEATH
A CHRISTIAN HANDBOOK ON LIVING AND DYING

iUniverse, Inc.

For information address:
iUniverse, Inc.
2021 Pine Lake Road, Suite 100
Lincoln, NE 68512
www.iuniverse.com

ISBN: 0-595-29452-9

Printed in the United States of America

This book is dedicated to four people who helped
to guide me on the road to developing my faith;
Sister Lillian for her evidence of grace
Judy Diedrich for her Gift of Patience
Monsignor Hayes for His Guidance,
And to Lou Vierra, for being my sponsor in faith.

Contents

PREFACE

Before you and I go forward in this book with this strange name, let me advise you to relax. Take a big deep breath, roll those shoulders, and exhale slowly. This read is really not going to be as difficult as you fear. I know, it is about that awful word, death. Sure, it does deal with dying and our need to prepare for that eventuality. I also agree that dying is probably not way up there on your can't wait to do list. It's not on mine either. But unless one of us finds a secret way of getting from here to there without that dying bit, die we must.

Why do I connect so much of this book to religion? Well, it reminds me of that old saying, "I've been rich and I've been poor, rich is better. I've been fat and I've been thin, liked thin better."

As a hospice volunteer I have watched people die with and without faith. With was better.

Will this book help you prepare for your death and live a fuller life even if you do not want the rest of the package? Yes it will. I cover issues and concerns and give you assistance and guidance that will ease the death process for you and your loved ones. I believe you will live a happier life with fewer regrets, and that will allow you to have a 'happier' death. It is my belief, however, that the development, and nourishment of our faith is a priceless tool in life and when we die.

So come on along with me, and let us walk this path together. Knowledge is power. We fear what we do not understand. Let us learn to live, live, fully, and the to die well.

PASSPORT

The God of all and everything, hereby requests that all whom it may concern permit this, his child, born on this earth, to pass without delay or hindrance, and when in case of need, give all faithful aid and protection.

ORIGIN: From where we all came and will return.

CURRENTLY RESIDES: On this earth

STATE: Hopeful

DESTINATION: Pending

DEPARTURE DATE: OPEN

CLASS OF TRAVEL DESIRED: First class

CONDITIONS: Traveler a little worried about the trip

SECTION 1: INTRODUCTION

OUR PRAYER

Did you know that our beloved Saint Joseph is the patron saint of the Universal Church?

The Catholic Church turns to Saint Joseph as the patron of families, of fathers, of social justice, of workers, and of the dying. There is even a special prayer to St. Joseph for what we all ultimately seek, A Happy Death.

"O glorious St. Joseph, behold I choose thee today for my special patron in my life and at the hour of my death. Preserve and increase in me the spirit of prayer and fervor in the service of God. Remove far from me every kind of sin; obtain for me that my death may not come upon me unawares, but that I may have time to confess my sins sacramentally and to bewail them with a most perfect understanding and a most sincere and perfect contrition, in order that I may breathe forth my soul to the hands of Jesus and Mary."

This prayer is a compassionate plea for being prepared for our death whenever it may comes.

Before we start on our voyage of preparation, let me share with you part of a Homily given by Monsignor Hayes of the St. Joseph Church in Los Banos, California. It is the story of a St. Charles Borromeo. It was said he was enjoying a game of cards with his friends one evening when the subject of death arose. What would you do, it was asked, if all of a sudden it were revealed to you that you were going to die that very night? There were various responses from the group. One would rush off to confession. Another would fall on his knees and frantically ask God's pardon and mercy. A more worldly answer came from one man who was perhaps more honest. He would dash off to his lawyer and check his will. But Saint Charles kept silent, looking at his cards. Eventually they realized he had not responded and the group asked him directly what he would do, His response was," I'd continue to play cards.

This story made me wonder how many of us spiritually, emotionally, financially, in any way, is that prepared?

The truth is, we are born to die. Life is a terminal disease.

It is an oxymoron that to live eternal life we must first die. That is a lot to accept, because we all kind of like this living thing we got goings. The thought of eternal life staggers our mind. It is a lot to comprehend, and to believe. Christians are told from childhood that we were given this gift of eternal life by Christ. HE paid for it with HIS death. A wise scholar once described faith and eternal life to me much like being offered the wedding invitation to attend a wedding feast. We can be invited, but we have to decide to attend, much like that proverbial horse that can be led to water but you can't make drink. God promises us eternal life is ours when we believe in him. HE gave us the free mind to accept or not to accept. We will die. If we are prepared is up to us.

I have seen firsthand many times the difference for both the dying, and their family when they are prepared. Prepared is better. Another area I address in the book is Regrets. Most of us have some regrets, and they can be very bitter. If we can live our life in a way that helps us dispose of some of those regrets, our life will be sweeter and our death easier. Then there is the wonderful freedom of forgiveness. Hate, grudges, and even the act of not carrying for others can be heavy burdens. Just think of poor of the ghost of old Jacob Marley in Dickens Christmas Carol. Jacob learned too late **what** he should have been doing during his time on earth. **Talk about taking your regrets and failures with you. Think of those heavy chains Marley dragged behind him in his** afterlife. **Marley's** gift to his friend Ebenezer Scrooge was more than the lessons of the three ghosts who taught him the true meaning of Christmas. They taught him a lot about the meaning of living a happy (good life).

As much as this is a book about our preparation for a Happy Death, how we live our life is so inter-twined with how we die; one cannot be considered without the other.

If we want to be surrounded by friends and loved ones at the time of our death, we must build those relationships during our life. If we want to have faith that will help us meet our death with peace and grace, (and get us into the heaven we seek) we need to seek out God while we are alive. Dinner cannot be served unless the food is bought, brought home, prepared and cooked. We cannot have our cake and eat it too. How we live, effects show we die.

1

DEALING WITH DEATH

"If YOU ARE NOT BUSY LIVING,
YOUR'RE BUSY DYING",

—BOB DYLAN

***In order* to face** death squarely we need to take away some cf its power. We need
to get it out of the closet and into the light of day. We can probably never really
understand death. It is beyond our capacity for explanation. We can go to a store
and try it on for size. There are no test drives for death. It is what it is and will
come when it will come. Our best hope is to study and try to prepare for the final
test. That we all will die makes our own death no less singular, or unique. We are
given our birth and our death like two slices of bread for a sandwich. Like at Subway, we decide how to fill in the middle.

We are all so different, and yet so much the same. We are born, we love, we
hurt, we laugh, we dream, we work, we strive, we love, we anger; we die. No getting away from it. What happens next is another question. The Sixty-Four Thou-
sand Dollar Question. The Final Answer. The Ultimate Survivor Challenge.
Have Faith, Will Travel.

The Bible tells us we are all bound by a shared heritage. We inherited the sen-
tence of death from Eve for her bite out of crime. We are told our heavenly
Father is loving, and forgiving parent, we are offered eternal life through Christ's
Salvation. If we want it.

The fact we die is our shared reality. I know it is said we must all face both
death and taxes. Oh, I know taxes can at times be creatively deferred, however
legally or ingeniously. Death has not yet met its match. If you do not take the
Passport to Heaven with faith in Christ, you are not going to win Final Jeopardy.
God may deliver us to his to heaven, but first we need to go through the gates of
death. I may desire heaven, but I can still fear death

I understand fear. I really would love to go to Europe some day. I dream of seeing the wonders of Scotland, Ireland, and England, I yearn to see the ancient castles, and to visit the museums filled with generations of art and artifacts. I can almost taste and smell the ethnic foods, BUT, I hate flying. The thought of that long plane ride over the Atlantic, the endless hours of confinement scares me to, well, death. It is not the destination I fear, it is the voyage. That is what death is too many. They want to get to the other side of it. It is just that 'darn dying' process in between.

Dying is not a popular process. Speaking of his attitudes on dying, W. C. Fields is known to have remarked," Personally, I would rather be in Philadelphia."

Our fear of the unknown is well expressed by Francis Bacon, "Men fear death, as children fear to go in the dark'.

It is that fear of the unknown, that exploration of that causes us to so fear death. Oh, we can picture heaven pretty well. We all have our own images of that eternal place. But that dying thing, well, as Woody Allen quipped, " I don't mind so much dying, I just don't want to be there when it happens."

For all of us death is always there waiting like that last day of summer vacation. It is that last piece of candy in the box of life. We have come to learn as we matured, that as long as those summers seemed in our youth, that last day came when we had to go back to school. We all learned the day would come when we would have to meet our new teachers, the new classmates and start all over again. As full of candy a box may seem, we learn that after we eat them, we are left with an empty box. As we have matured, we have learned that while the heavens may be are infinite, most things were not. Like our time on earth.

Do you remember when you first realized you were mortal? When you figured out someday you would die. It was quite a shock wasn't it? As sure as the sun rises and sets, we grow older, and death is something we need to learn to face. We need to accept the fact that our own death is the unavoidable bill that will come at the end of our life's banquet.

People have been talking about death since it all began. Way back in 1662 in 'The Book of the Dead', it is written, "In the midst of life we are in death." It consoles us with this promise,

"Earth to earth, ashes to ashes, dust to dust in the sure and certain hope of the resurrection unto eternal life."

Now, I love that eternal life thing, I really do. I'm banking my whole life on it. BUT, it's that ashes bit that scares me. How can we not think about it? When I worry I think to myself, What if I am not ready yet? What if I am only half way through painting the house? What if I haven't been good enough? What if I forgot to take out the garbage, or left the iron on? What if no one knows what I want? What if I forgot to get things cleared up with God first? (The ultimate, oops) What if??

I have a confession to make. I read the obituaries for two reasons. Sure, I am checking to see if there is the name of anyone I know, but also to make sure my name isn't there? And I'm always relieved when it isn't. We know that death so far has a perfect score. No one has made it out of this life alive. But aren't you secretly wishing that maybe you will be the first? If only Houdini had come back like he promised and could tell us all for sure. That would sure help. We know Lazarus came back, but he didn't share any secrets. (BUT JESUS DID) So many, millions, billions of others, have traveled the road from life to death. Not one has sent back postcards. It is only through the bible that we are given a hint of the heaven we may find on the other side of the veil. It (our death) is a trip we all must make alone. We can go with our bags packed with faith and trust in our eternal life, or we can go with no faith in our suitcase. But, but go we will.

So dear friend, if we must die, let us have what we prayed to St. Joseph for. Let us have a happy death. Let us shame death and face it with faith, preparation, style, grace and yes, even some humor.

It may seem an oxymoron, this term a happy death. But if we look up the word Happy in the Webster's dictionary these words are listed as definition; fortunate, fitting, CONTENT. WE can be content at our death. Things can be done 'fittingly', and wouldn't that be fortunate?

We can, by thinking, praying about, and preparing for our death, have it more the 'Burger King' our way."

If you had no choice about how came you into this world, you sure can have a say in how you go out. And in the style we choose. This time no economy seat for you. You want to go first class. As is said in our passport at the beginning of this book, for most of us the date of our departure is unknown. Death, for most of us, comes unawares. Still we don't need to be helpless to the mighty sickle carried by the grim reaper. We can be like the trustworthy boy or girl scout, and be prepared There are things we can do to help us face the financial, legal, emotional, spiritual, price tags that come with death.

The purpose of this book is to be a multi-dimensional death primer, a handbook to help you through life into death. Not all situations may pertain to your particular situation. It is my sincere hope that these pages will offer you insights, information, and inspiration to guide you on your final journey. I hope it will help with the mental, emotional, spiritual, financial, and legal and ritual of the process that is your last voyage. This book's goal is to give the reader a comprehensive study of how one can prepare for, 'A Happy Death'.

We do not live alone on this earth, and our death affects others. In Frank Capra's Christmas film, 'It's a Wonderful Life', the story tells how a man learned that his life had affected other's lives profoundly. The main character played, so memorably by Jimmy Stewart, had no idea how many people he had touched in his brief journey on earth. We are all like that fictional character. We do not fully comprehend how our profoundly our life, and therefore, our death may affect others. Death leaves a mark, and a makes a history all of its own. We must face death and prepare for it.

I was told the story of two magicians. They were always in tremendous competition with each other, and always tried to out do the other with a more creative trick. This rivalry went on for years. Each magician became more and more daring and creative with their conjuring. At last, one of the two became gravely ill. The magician called his competition to his deathbed. The ill man whispered for his competitor to bend closer, "Now watch as I do the ultimate trick before your eyes. Watch me disappear." Then the man closed his eyes and died.

Perhaps that is what we fear the most about death. The fear we will loose our identity. The fear we will be forgotten.

We are so used to being US. Why everywhere we go, there we are. If we are nervous visiting a strange country where we do not know the language and customs, it is understandable that death might make us a bit ill at ease. Death is not considered normally as a happy subject. In fact, it can really kill a person's sense of humor.

William Shakespeare may have said," A rose by any other name would smell as sweet". Well I say, death by any other name, demised, expired, vacated, life challenged, kaput, well, is still the end of our time on earth.

Just what is Death anyway? Let's get technical for a moment. The definition in Webster is "the extinction of life; manner of dying; state of being dead, termination, dissolution." Dead is defined in the same test as "without life." Well, what is Life? Webster defines it as existence; vitality; the span between life and death.' Today even those definitions are challenged as scientific advances have created an artificial life-extending environment. Many today have been challenged to rethink their views on life and of dying .The fourth edition of Black's Law Dictionary carried the following version of the classic definition of death, "Death: The cessation of life; the ceasing of life to exist; defined by physicians as a total stoppage of the circulation of the blood and a cessation of the animal and vital functions consequent thereupon, such as respirators, pulsation, etc."

How do our spiritual leaders define death? Pope, Pius XII, responded in a speech to an International Congress of Anesthesiologists, held in November of 1957, "The church's concept of death is the complete and final separation of the soul from the body." "However," he also said, "it remains for the doctor, and especially the anesthesiologist, to give a clear and precise definition of 'death' and the 'moment of death' of a patient who passes away in a state of unconsciousness."

Two leading American Roman Catholic pro-life philosophers, Germain Grisez and Joseph Boyle, concluded, "Death is the irreversible loss of integrated organic functioning."

American Dr. Robert Troug, director of the multi disciplinary intensive care unit at Harvard Medical School, defines Death, as "Death is the irreversible loss of the capacity for conscious."

Let's consider the Chairman of the Harvard Brain Death Committee Henry Beechers' statement in his address to the American Association for the Advancement of Science, "That what is essential to human nature is 'the individual's personality, his conscious life, his uniqueness, his capacity for remembering, judging, reasoning, acting, enjoying, worrying, and so on."

Does any of that help? The reality for us is, no matter what the scientific or theological definition, is dead is when We cease to exist HERE. I have always loved the definition of life as a terminal disease, sexually transmitted. We may as well laugh at death. We cannot capture it, but by faith we sure can conquer it.

You would think we would have gained some philosophical sophistication by now with the subject of death. We see it every day in our living room on television. Movies have made slow motion death an art form. The most popular video games make the players master killers. One of today's most popular television programs is CSI. This detective shows uses forensics to help find the killer. This program has shown us ways we can die we could never have even imagined. Every day reminders of death surround us. A lot of us just adjust our tunnel vision glasses, and prefer not to think about it. The death of others deaths is hard enough to imagine; ours, almost impossible.

Philosophers have always dealt with the challenge of death.

Richard John Neuhaus writes in his insuring book, 'As I Lay', " Not that death is the purpose of our being born, but we are born toward death, and in each of our lives the work of dying is already under way. The work of dying well, is in large part, the work of living well."

I couldn't have said it any better. For the reality now, is the same as it was in 1662, in Burial of the Dead, " In the mid0st of life, we are in death."

Simone De Beawair wrote of death in her work of 1970 'Coming of Age', " And indeed it is old age, rather than death that is to be contrasted to life. Old age is life's parody, whereas death transforms life into a destiny. In a way, death preserves life by giving it the absolute dimension, as unto himself eternity changes him at last Death does away with time."

Really, we wouldn't want to live forever on earth. We just don't want to die now.

A great example of our changing attitudes towards death is the highly popular HBO Series,

—Six Feet Under'. The televised scenes of caskets, funerals, embalming rooms, and wild variety of ways we can come to face our death have become great drama, and at times, great humor. In one episode a niece, very emotionally distraught over the sudden death of her beloved Aunt, demands of one of the young morticians," Why do people have to die?"

The mortician, who had recently himself been diagnosed with a potentially terminal condition, showed great thought before he gave his simple, yet complex answer, " To make life matter."

Some Christians, who possess a strong faith, may even feel guilty to admit that they have any fear of their death. They may me feel it shows alack of faith in Gods promise. Yet, the fear of the unknown is a very natural and human emotion

Some people fear their death so much they live less a life. They carry their fear of death to an almost paralyzing degree and in the process miss so much of what life has to offer.

Dennis Wholey reflected in his book, 'When the Worst That Can Happen Already, Has,' "The subject of death is fraught with denial. Our own mortality is terribly threatening for us to acknowledge on an emotion level. How we will die is frightening to most of us. We struggle with the question, is this all there is?"

If we can learn to lessen the fear and guilt, and death on a healthier level, we will live a happier and more productive life. We will also face our death with fewer regrets. I know this is a lot to swallow and have to accept. But, death is the ultimate lesson in acceptance. It is the perfect definition for the popular bumper sticker,—Let Go, and Let God.'

Those blessed with the gift of faith can see the heaven as the light at the end of the tunnel. Faith gives us hope. Faith gives us a reason to believe death is not an ending, but a transition. This makes developing ones faith a very desirable goal.

Let's get out our broom, and open the windows, and sweep some fears away. Let us take death out of the closet.

2

DEALING WITH THE EMOTIONS

♦

LOSS, MOURNING, GRIEF AND CLOSURE

Life is full of many wonderful moments of joys and laughter. There are times we are so over the top happy we feel like we are on top of the world. We are, we say, in Seventh Heaven. But as my beloved Mother in Law would often say, " Nothing is so or so bad that it lasts forever." That means we have a price to pay for those high highs with low lows. When we open ourselves up to the wonder of loving others, we also open ourselves to the pain of loss. All of our lives will be touched by the painful, but necessary emotions of loss, mourning, and grief. We all will have times when we will have to deal with those emotions. We will need to fond some peace and closure.

I know it is so hard to let go of anything we love. I hate to throw out even a faded birthday card or an old drawing done by one of my children. Loosing a person is almost intolerable. The sure knowledge that we will have to endure these losses does not help them hurt less.

This old Quaker prayer speaks of the process.

"We give them back to you, dear Lord,
Who gaveth them to us.
Yet as thou didst not loose them in giving.
So we have not lost them by their return.

For what is thine, is ours always if we are thine.
And life is eternal and love is immortal,

And death is only a horizon, and a horizon is nothing more
Than the limit of our sight."

I have heard many times that it is in times of crisis great courage is born. Well, we are never more challenged than when struck by the sword of grief. The bible tells us "Blessed are they that mourn for they shall be comforted."

It is sometimes hard to accept that when we are in the throes of pain. Yet, we are told in faith that God is never closer or more ready too ease our burden, than at those times. Just as our parents tried to comfort us when we were hurt, God the Father desires to comfort us.

Part of the price of living and loving is that pain of loss. When we loose something we hold dear, be it our life, or another's, we mourn. Because we are not perfect, we will regret. Because we should not suffer without end, there must be closure.

Bishop Sheen said, "Shall we place our joys in time or in eternity, for we cannot have them both. Shall we mourn before we die, or after we die? For we cannot mourn both. We cannot have our reward on earth and on heaven."

Sometimes it is very hard to remember, and comprehend, that those we hold most dear, never truly leave us. They live on in the kindness they showed, the comfort they shared, and the love they brought into our lives. It is hard to believe, when we are hurting, that they are in a better place. We want them with us. It is hard to accept that it is to late to say we love someone one more time, to say we are sorry, or to undo what we meant always to undo. These are hard, painful truths. We know that our Christ's last words were of acceptance, pure faith and trust when he uttered, "Father into your hands I commend my spirit."

We are in awe of his divine acceptance. But, we are just learning. God, we are trying. But at times, when it hurts so badly, we don't know what to do.

This makes me think of a story a dear friend of mine told of her beloved father in law. This man was from the old country, very stoic in nature, was dying of cancer. A strong man of faith, he was suffering greatly from the very worse that cancer can do. Cancer can do terrible things. My friend watched her father in law as his pain became more and more intense. He valiantly strived to deal with the suffering he had been given. One morning he was particularly distraught, and my friend asked him what was the matter. He cried he was filled it guilt and ashamed of himself. He told her he had such a wonderful family and he knew the Lord had given him so much to live for. Yet, he admitted, earlier in the day, he had sobbed out of weakness from the pain, and had prayed to die. He was so disappointed in himself. His faith told him those thoughts were a sin. He loved his family and wanted to live for them. My friend soothed away his distress and comforted him. He died shortly after.

Sometimes we can only say, " God we know what we need to do, but sometimes it is hard. But we are trying."

We learn by example. Unfortunately, sometimes we just look to the wrong person for an example. Jesus showed us the perfect way, but His are pretty big footsteps to follow. Psychotherapist, Irvin Yalon, in his work in—Loves Executioner', stated he felt that the way one faces ones death (and logically the death of others) is determined by the model one's parents set. I believe that we are a collection of all our life experiences. That it is never more true than when dealing with the subject of death. If we have been raised to keep the subject of death as a taboo topic, only whispered about, it is natural these emotions carry over into our mature years.

Customs have changed. In the past, funeral vigils were held in the family homes. The casket of the loved one was kept in a place of honor in the parlor. Death was treated as a natural part of life. Families and friends gathered together in strength and comfort, helping each other to go on. Did this closer contact with the reality of death make loss easier? Someone who is often exposed to an illness develops resistance. Perhaps, it did at least take away some of the mystique. Still, there is no easy, pain free way to short circuit grief. We all need to go through the stages. In fact, it is unhealthy to NOT go through the very real and necessary steps of dealing with loss. However, there are ways to make it easier to deal with the process. There are ways we can learn to reach out, and to help cope better with the necessary process.

One of things that does help is to free our mind of useless, harmful emotional clutter. Those years of anger, resentments, grudges, hurt feelings, and wishes for revenge can take up a lot of energy. With all that negative energy, there is not much room left for the good, healthy kind. One helpful tool is called closure.

Closure is so important to the human psyche that nurses in hospice and hospital floors who deal with the dying, say that patients with 'unfinished business' to do will hang on in desperation to see it finished. Those who are unable to do so seem to pass on in a lesser state of peace, and to even experience more pain. Closure is the process of acceptance. It is the mental closing of a door in our lives. True closure means we have made peace with an issue or experience. Closure means we are ready to move on with our lives, a loss, or our death. Many marriage counselors agree that the reason for the failure of many second marriages is the unsettled business of the first. It is hard for us to move on with anything when part of us still has a foot in the other door.

We need to completely move out of our old house before they we can move into the new, metaphorically speaking. Life and Death are like that. We do not want to move all that destructive garbage along with us. We need to take it to the mental dump and be free of its contamination.

So can we learn to deal with closure? I have an exercise I share with groups when I speak. For this simple exercise we will need to make two lists. Be prepared to have some of your emotions stirred up, but this is good aerobic emotional exercise. Good for your heart, and good for your soul. You are going to sleep much better.

The first list we title with that big R word, REGRETS. Ouch. I hate them. All those, if only's, and could have, should have, would haves, which mess up our sleep too many nights. We all have said and done something's we have regretted afterwards. That just comes with breathing. If this chapter helps you fix or release one regret, help close one door, then your way to a happy death is made that much easier. So make your list now of regrets. No one else is going to read it, so be honest. Sorry you gossiped about your neighbor" Do you regret you didn't tell Max you were sorry? Does it haunt you that you didn't help you brother when he was sick? Does it bother you that you have stopped going to church? Write each regret down. Get rid of each and every one of those nasty things. They are doing you no good. Face em, name em.

Now what? One sure fire way to help with closure and regrets is PRAYER. Prayer is the ultimate source of closure. Nothing works soothing regrets quite like a talk 'one on one' with the master of Counselors. Many Catholics feel that in their rite of reconciliation. They are blessed by that bowed head, asking for forgiveness, and freely accepting HIS mercy. We can all experience that cool shower of spiritual blessing and cleansing. It is the ultimate answer. Still, an Emotional Closet Cleaning can be a very therapeutic thing at any step of your life. So we are going to take this list of things we are feeling badly about, words said, deeds done, and determine which are fixable, and which need to become releasable. The idea of the list is to help you find out what you would like to say or do to, to give you that much sought after closure, right here and now. Why put off to death what you can do today? Think of how freeing it will be to have this hard work done.

Let GO and Let GOD. Sometimes we will have to accept that's something cannot be undone. For these items, and I am sure we all have some of those, letting go is the only form of closure we can receive. We have to learn to be able to separate the I can fix it and darn if I won't, and the I have to learn to live with this one, but I'll never do it again, type of regrets. I am sure we all can immediately think of one of many of those moments. Mine are legion. My brother and I had exchanged heated, stormy words. I felt I had every reason to justify my continued anger. I mean the best kind of justifiable, you would feel the same way too, reasons to not talk with him. Days turned into weeks, weeks into months, and life went on until I received that terrible call telling me of his death. There are not words descriptive enough to tell you how much I wish I had a chance to talk to him one more time. Regret. Yeah, big time. I have prayed about it. Have I learned from it? Yes. Have I pledged to never let anything like that happened again? Yes. Has it caused me to tell others to let anger go, and mend those old torn down fences? You betcha. Closure can come in a variety of colors. The way to deal with this kind of regret has to be acceptance and a lesson learned to benefit future behavior

Now there are some regrets that are fixable. The person is alive and you can call them, write them and undo. The basic twelve step programs, which are so successful for many, stresses the benefits of making amends.

Your other regret list is much more fun. This Regret list has to do with hope and opportunities. It is for the other kind of regrets. The wish I had kind. The, I wish I had climbed that mountain, gone back to school, learned how to fly fish, or ate caviar for breakfast kind of regrets. I want you to put on your best day dreaming headdress and go to town now. Think big, think small, but think about what you have always wanted to do, and not done.

If one of the things you always wanted to do is travel, is that possible? Perhaps you can begin small by watching travel channels, attending Travel films at your local community college, or get a tape and learn a foreign language. Then go see a film from that country and be able to understand it without the sub-titles. If you always wanted to go to Europe, and there is not enough time or money, find a small community near by that shares some of its customs. Solvang in California for the Danish, Holland, Michigan for the Dutch, or Chinatowns are in many large cities. Always wanted to go to England? Tea Rooms are popping up all over and give you a transcontinental experience for an hour or so, at a bargain price and no jet lag.

Next. Oh this one is like a Christmas list for Santa when you were little and you wanted the big fire engine, and marshmallows for dinner every night. This list will help you find the things that mean the most to you, that bring you joy. If you only had one week left to live, how would you want to fill your days? These lists will help you live happier now. They will also allow you to die with less regret, then. Go ahead, the sky is the limit (maybe you always wanted to sky dive??) dream and make those lists.

Ok, another fun and very healthy exercise. Be your travel agent and describe in vivid detail, first a perfect week, and then a perfect day. I want you to be very specific. What would you eat? Drink? What would you wear? What music would you listen to? Who would you want to spend that time with?

Now go over the list again. Tell yourself this is your last week on this earth. Your last day. What would you choose to do and surround yourself with if you could direct this final exit? Keep this list and reread it whenever you can. Who were the people you wanted to spend those last hours with? What did you eat? Where did you go? What music did you play? What sights, what picture would you try to capture? NOW, do these things every chance you can. Put at least one of those things in everyday. Any day could be your last 24 hours. Now you know what you would do, do it. Remember a Happy Death is as free of regrets and "if only's" as possible.

Now on to the very difficult, painful, unavoidable subject of loss and grief. Life is a balancing act of joys, happiness and positive experiences along with the difficult and painful. We are told in the Bible verse Ecc. 3:1-11, " There is an appointed time for everything, and a time for every affair under the heavens. A time to be born, and a time to die, a time to weep, and a time to laugh; a time to mourn, and a time to dance, a time to love and a time to hate."

I admire the inner strength of the famed poet Wordsworth, "We will grieve not, rather find strength in what remains behind."

No matter how strong our faith, or strong of character, the emotional crosses of loss and grief are still difficult burdens to bear. This is true for the loss of someone we love. It is true as we prepare for the ultimate loss of our own life. Some of the tools needed to deal with both losses are the same. One cannot prepare for a Happy Death without dealing with the four-letter word of loss. Having feelings of loss and grief does not mean that we possess little faith. It does not mean that we doubt that those we lost have gone on to a happier existence with God. Grief and loss are very normal, human emotions. There is not a capsule that you can take with a glass of orange juice, go to bed and awaken the next morning grief free. If I could create one I could retire for life in luxury. But, there are some tools that can help you come to terms with grief.

First, while you are suffering from grief take extra special care of yourself. Your getting sick or sicker, does not help the pain, it compiles it As Madeline Engle wisely said in her book—Two-Part Invention', " We pull ourselves together when we need to. We have things that have to be done. But we need to give ourselves times and places to mourn. This is strength, not weakness."

This is a time you need to allow others help you. Turn to others for support. They want to help. It is a grace to allow them to help. It is OK to cry, to rave, anything you feel, is ok. The emotions we feel are ours. Talk to your friends, your doctors, counselors, your Priest or minister. Seek out support groups. Use any shoulder. You need to heal. Let others help, and PRAY. God is always awake. I have a sign above my bed given to me by a dear friend, that reads, " Before you go to sleep, turn your problems over to God, He is going to be up all night anyway." It really helps

After my mother died, I was filled with grief for a long time. One night I was especially upset thinking about how I would never see her again. Then it hit me. I would see her again. When it was time. It made me feel better to remember that promise. I still miss her every day, but it gives me great comfort to remember we will be reunited.

The following word words have also brought me comfort when dealing with loss. They come from—Darkness Visible' by William Styron, " For those who have dwelt in depressions dark wood, and known its inexplicable agony, their return from the abyss is not unlike the ascent of the poet, trudging upward, and upward out of hell's black depths and at last emerging into what he saw as—the shining world.' There, whoever has been restored to health has almost always been restored to the capacity for serenity and joy, and this may indemnity enough for having endured the despair beyond despair. And so we came forth, and once more again beheld the stars."

Of course, there is no simple, pat answer for people struck with loss. There does seem, however, to be a pattern that loss, and grief seems to follow. There are necessary stages that most people travel in the healing process. The first, and by far the hardest step, is acceptance. A person has to come to terms with the reality of the loss. Each person comes to accept the loss in his or her own time. Acceptance can be a mighty mountain to climb. There may be times when all we feel is sadness, when the world is a melancholy blur of tears, and sorrow. There will be a time when there is numbness, a strange sensation of almost being a spectator to your life's drama. Then there is the disbelief, a sense of unreality; a great incredulity that this is possible. Ah and lets not forget that red head of anger. Anger shows its head and makes you to rant at the heavens, why? In whatever order they may come to you, they are all normal. They are a part of the process

Another real emotion we have to deal with is the sting of guilt. You may feel Survivors' guilt if you are the one left behind. You may feel guilty wishing it were someone else who had died, or were dying. Often when we learn we are dying we feel guilty about leaving our loved ones behind. This is especially true of parents who worry about leaving their children, or a spouse who is very protective. These people fear they are letting their loved ones down with their death. It can be hard to accept the fact that things just happen, with out fault or blame.

People die. We will. When it is our time. In the hauntingly beautiful movie,—House of Spirits', Meryl Streep's portrays a wife and mother who returns from the dead to deliver two completely different messages. Messages about—when it is time'. First, the Mother appears to her daughter, portrayed by Winona Ryder. Ryder's character has been beaten and raped, while held captive in a cold, dreary cell. She is ready to surrender to her pain, agony, and despair. She began to seek death as a form of escape from the reality of her condition. Then, Streep mystically enters the cell, dropping to the cold, concrete floor. Gently placing her daughter's head on her lap, cradling her with affection, she strokes her hair. She admonishes Ryder not to give in, nor to wish for her death, however tempting it may be. The Mother whispers to her daughter, " Do not wish for death, my love, for it will come to you one day. But today is not the day." But she admonishes her that her granddaughters' needs her mother back, and for Ryder to fight hard to come back. These words of spiritual comfort and encouragement are effective, and Ryder survives.

Later in the film Streep' s ghost makes an appearance to her husband. He is shown lying on his bed, obviously not feeing well. Suddenly tears well up in his eyes as he sees his beloved, deceased wife kneel beside him. She strokes his hair. Her eyes filled with love, and compassion she sooths him as he closes his eyes and joins her in the afterlife. For him, it was time.

Everyone deals with grief in his or her own time, and in their own way. You do not have to appear strong. Talk. Listen. Accept the support offered you. Some people who find it acceptable to acknowledge the grief they have felt over losing someone else; fail to recognize we go through the same processes when we face the reality of our own death.

Elisabeth Kubler Ross wrote the definitive book on this subject with her groundbreaking,—On Death and Dying' which defines the stages of dealing with grief. Ross defined these stages as denial, anger, bargaining, depression and acceptance. Ross believes that all these stages seem to play themselves out, though not always in that specific order. With my research for both of my books on death, I have spoken to many people who have been given a terminal diagnosis, as well as their families. They all seemed to share these same symptoms as they came to deal with their acceptance of death. Different order, but same symptoms. The GOOD NEWS, the one big overwhelming, deciding factor in all I have spoken to is, those with a firm faith have a better transition. Those dying with faith displayed less fear, and remarkably, often less pain.

To help with the grieving process (and, also help our fears of being forgotten after we die) I believe we need to remember that those we hold most dear, never truly leave us. They live on in the kindness they showed, the comfort they shared, and the love they brought into our lives. It has amazed me each time I have lost someone how suddenly I am able to see them so vividly in my minds eye. I can hear their voice, their words as if they have climbed inside my conscious mind, and have become a part of me. It is very comforting, and is in itself, a form of immortality.

Now lets deal with another useful exercise for closure, healing, and dealing with loss.

LETTING GO: Preparing to say goodbye

This is a lesson on goodbyes that will help with your passage—then', but also help with your living now. This is something I believe is so valuable that I repeat this lesson as often as I can with those I council on death and dying. They are the goodbye letters. The idea of the good-bye letters was born from an old episode of Marcus Welby M.D., a popular medical show way before the days of ER. The famous father figure of Father Knows Best, Robert Young, portrayed the physician with the winning bedside manner. I enjoyed this caring and compassionate program. I learned many valuable life's lessons as the drama revealed itself each week. All the programs were good, but one show stands out in memory for the lesson it taught me. This episode told the story of a young woman, well portrayed by Susan Clark, who suffered from terrible headaches. After tests diagnosed her with inoperable brain cancer, Clark's character rode the many emotions of such a diagnosis from disbelief, to great anger. She became so overcome with anger that she pushed people away from her at the time she really needed them most. Clark built up walls made of rage and self-pity, and climbed inside herself. Finally, the doctors were able to reach Clark with this message, "You have been given a gift that many people wish they had been given, the gift of time. You have been given the opportunity to say good-bye. A chance to say you are sorry, to set the record straight. You can hug that person one more time, see the sunset and enjoy it as only one who knows how precious they are, can see it. You can leave a legacy. You can write to everyone who ever mattered to you. With no fear of regret, tell them from your heart how you feel. You can do all this, because God has given you the time. The time to say good-bye."

This message resonated with Clark. One by one, she wrote her letters of love and appreciation to others. Each letter, a blessing to those who received them, also helped to create a peace and grace for the dying character. She had been given the gift to finally tell so many she cared for how much they had touched her life. Each letter enriched her with cherished memory, and also freed her. The process brought her happiness and peace. How many people are there in your life you would want to write such a letter to? Perhaps a teacher who made such a difference, a neighbor who was always there, a find you have lost touch with? Think of all the words you plan to say, in that elusive world of—someday.' We will tell them, show them, do this for them, go on that trip, read that book, go back to school, and look up at the stars all,—someday.' This project made such a difference for the character, and all those who received the letters. Fiction? Yes. But, the lesson is real, and one we all can benefit from. There is a section in your Workbook for your Goodbye letter list. Keep your lists of your perfect weekend and day there as well. Reread them. Use them. Use them then, but also use them Now. Sometimes—someday' is sooner than you think.

Another valuable tool is what I call Our Shower Journal. This is another one of the projects I often recommend for those who are in the dying process, or who have someone they care for dying. There is just something about a shower that makes many people loosen up. We can sing in that shower like they we could never anywhere else. It can be a good place to yell and vent our anger or tears. W e feel a freedom to express ourselves under the water spray where no one else is around to hear your frustrations, (or your singing off key). We feel freer to express ourselves without fear of judgment. Your Shower Journal is not only a good emotional health tool, it can be a beautiful gift for those left behind. This journal is a place where you can release those thoughts and fears, vent that anger, ask those questions of why, scream in protest, and cry with pain. It can also be where you count your blessings, recall your dreams, and list the wishes of your heart. Just remember that the main reason for you to write is just to vent and clear your head, and heal your heart. If you want the journal destroyed later, just instruct so, or leave it to someone you love as a testimony of your feelings at the time. It is recommended by many in the mental health field to use a journal. I have journaled for as long back as I can remember. Confronting your last chapter of life, it can be a gift to yourself as well as to those we leave behind.

Another from of journal that can be very beneficial is Prayer Journal. It can be a real blessing as well as a great faith-building tool. In a prayer journal we can communicate with God, share our concerns, our fears and our praise. Our Lord is the ultimate counselor, the greatest comforter. Turning to him in prayer, written or oral, is always a prescription for good spiritual health whatever our stage of life. A prayer journal is also a good place to write quotations or prayers that bring you comfort and strength. This prayer journal can become a resource as well as a source of refuse.

TO LIVE A HAPPY LIFE HELPS LEAD TO A HAPPY DEATH WITH FEWER REGRETS: Now, it's time to consider this banquet of life we are given on earth. Some people savor much its richness, feeding well at the table of experience life. Other people barely graze through life, gently nibbling but never really enjoying all that life has to offer. To understand loss better, and to appreciate what we have now in life more, we have another exercise. This exercise in loss will help you appreciate all you have. For this beneficial activity we need to tune into all our five senses. We need to rediscover how each one helps to enrich our lives. As you become reacquainted with these wonderful, tactile, sensual messengers, experiment as to what causes you pleasure. Do you feel calmer with the scent of vanilla? Does the taste of custard make you feel safe with memories of childhood? Do you feel happier dressed in yellow? Do you work better to big band music? Embrace your senses and their contribution to your Happy Life. Fill them with a joyful passion. Soak them in; revel in these gifts from God so that they will be well spent at the time of your death. Now that you are more keenly in touch with your gift of sense, it is time to go on to the exercise. List these senses on a piece of paper. Now, one by one, scratch one from the list. Do so in order of what you feel you would miss the least. Sound, smell, sight, taste, and touch. One by one remove one. Soon they are all gone. These are real losses. For those of us facing death, this is part of the loss, part of our fear. Now think! NOW you have those senses. Feed them, revel in them, they are great gifts. Enjoy and praise God for the bounty of richness that each of these senses gives to our daily life.

For the next step take a sheet of paper and pencil and start listing all your likes: foods, music, places, holidays, material possessions, friends, and relatives. It will not take you long to have a very long list. Now, like with your list of senses, start taking one thing off at a time. As you take things off your list, the decisions become harder, more painful. Still, you need to keep taking away, one treasured thing or person at a time. What can you live without? You grow sadder as you see these precious things disappear. This is how it can seem to a person who is dying. BUT, they are yours NOW! Hold those gifts dear, drink them in!

And yet another list. This list is all about you. I want you to write all the things you like about yourself. Is it your hair, your chin, your smile, your dance steps? Now take a trait away, one at a time. What would you wish to lose last? These are real losses. NOW realize that while you read this all these things are yours. Everything on all of your lists is a precious thing you possess. The real secret of a Happy Death is to live your life well. Look at your lists often, especially when you are down. Remind yourself just how rich your life is. God gave us life to live fully. We should savor and enjoy every minute of his gift of earth. The true loss is to not enjoy it NOW!

A NATIVE AMERICAN PRAYER

"I give you this one thought to keep, I am with you still, I do not sleep "Do not think of me as gone, I am with you still, in each new dawn."

3

FOLLOW THE LEADER;
LEARNING FROM OTHERS

◆

DEATHS AND WORDS

"Afraid! Of whom am I afraid?
Not death, for who is he?
The Porter of my fathers lodge
As much abasheth me
Because I could not stop for death
He kindly stopped for me
The carriage held just ourselves,
and immortality.
I never spoke with God
Nor visited in heaven
Yet certain am I of the spot
As if the checks were given."
Emily Dickinson 1830–18886

I wish I had the complete and unshakable peace and confidence expressed in this famous poem. When we need encouragement, inspiration, or a comforting word, the experience of others can be of great aid. This chapter will consider the thoughts, words and deed of others on death.

Simon De Beawair, in Coming of Age, expressed of death that, " There is no such thing as a natural death; nothing that happens to a man is ever natural; since his presence calls the world into question' All men must die, but for every man his death is an accident, an unjustifiable violation."

"Death is no more a defeat than is growing taller, starting school, or falling in love. All are phases of life, and each brings with it a special set of hazards and satisfactions. To live with grace we must be prepared to live with grace," are the inspiring words of Arnold Beisser in 'A Graceful Passage'.

We have already dealt with the necessity of accepting death. That we all must die, we know, if not accept. Just as we wish to do well at school or to excel in anything we attempt, we all hope to live well and to die with dignity. We hope that people will say of us, " They died well".

As Sherwin Nuland says in his How We Die, " The dignity we create in the time allotted to us becomes a continuum with the dignity we achieve by the altruism of accepting the necessity. To most people, death remains a hidden secret, as erotic zed as feared. We are irresistibly attracted by the anxieties we find most terrifying; we are drawn to them by a primitive excitement that a rises from flirtation with danger. Moths and flames; mankind and death, there is little difference."

Perhaps that explains our societal love of horror films and depictions of graphic deaths.

When I think of the theme of grace and acceptance in connection with death I often recall a scene from an old Charlton Heston film called—Soy lent Green'. Because of the over population of the world of the future depicted in the movie, older or ill people were encouraged to commit suicide. A special building of sanctuary was built for this purpose. In the film, the new world is a cold and barren place where there are no longer flowers, forest or so many of the natural beauties we enjoy today. They have all been lost to over population. After a person consents to—move on and make room' they are rolled into a large room and as they are about to be given their—farewell injection', a film is shown on a large screen showing the majesty of our old planet earth. In a painfully poignant scene the classic actor Edward G Robinson is brought in to see the movie, and to die. A long, slow close up of his face is shown as his eyes see, for the first time, such beauty. Tears of sheer joy cross his face. It was a tremendously moving scene. The scene had an even greater impact on me when later I learned of Edward G Robinson's death, and that he had known his prognosis when he acted in the film. Robinson was keenly aware of the value of all his senses, and how they enriched his life. As I always say on any particularly beautiful day, God does good work.

I have had the honor of dealing with many people as they have faced their death. I have been repeatedly impressed with the dignity of the human spirit. Just the other day another friend died, after a prolonged illness. Drawing on her faith, strength and love of her family, she faced those last months with a quiet resolve. She used the time to make all her own arrangements, settling issues and spent real quality time with those she loved. It (knowing she was soon to die) almost seemed to free her from worrying about, what she now knew to be unimportant things. She centered her mind and thoughts on what really mattered. She felt her last few months to be a gift. Watching her last steps on this journey through life was a gift for all those who were privileged to know her.

One of my favorite true stories tells of a woman who knew she was dying. This woman was actively involved in every detail of her funeral plans. She had always been an organized and take-charge type of person. She certainly was not leaving her death to anyone else's care. She had her pastor over and had him write down every detail. She chose the psalms to be read, the hymns to be sung, her pallbearers, and planned the menu to be served at the wake. At last, satisfied she had dealt with all the issues, she dismissed her pastor to return to his church. Just as he was about to reach the door, she shouted out for him to return. She said she had almost forgotten a very important detail. She instructed him she wanted a fork placed in her hand in her casket. The pastor looked at his parishioner with concern. Perhaps she was delirious. Noting his confusion, the woman made this inspiring explanation," At all our wonderful parish dinners, when we are finished eating, and they come to take away our plates, we are always told to hold on to our forks. That always makes me smile because I knew that a great dessert is coming next. I hope that when people come to my funeral, and see the fork in my hand; it will make people ask why it is there. Then you can explain it is because I knew something great is coming next."

How will we react when we are told it is our time? No one really knows. Each year over 250, 000 people learn they have a terminal illness. The quality of that quantity of life left is determined by the answer to this question," Do they want to spend the rest of your time dying or living?' I do not know the author of these words, "We cannot look at the sun all the time, nor can we look at death all the time." To me they are profound. They speak to the artful balance we need in preparation for death by being a wise steward, and still a joyful child.

As we all enter the world, we all must exit, each in our own way. I love the last remarks of the writer Oscar Wilde. Wilde looked around his deathbeds room, scowled at the wallpaper and said, with his razor sharp wit, " Either the wallpaper or I have to go. " And then he died. Talk about a great exiting line.

We are told that when Martin Luther King was dying, he repeated three times, "Into thy hands I commend my spirit! Thou hast redeemed me, O God of truth."

How wonderful that he was able to face his sudden death with such grace, and complete confidence in his redeemer. Since death so often takes us unawares, isn't it good to have your faith ready as a shield?

We can learn a lot about a man from his last words. John Milton's farewell was filled with hope and anticipation, "Death is the great key that opens the palace of eternity."

Ben Hur's author, Lew Wallace, last words were of peace and acceptance, "Thy will be done." What perfect acceptance.

These words of no less a words smith than William Shakespeare tell of his strong faith, " I commend my soul into the hands of God my creator, hoping and assuredly believing, through the merits of Jesus Christ my savior, to be made partaker of life ever lasting and my body to the earth, whereof it is made." Faith personified.

HOW IT WENT; I am going to share now with you a few examples of how some met their death. Our first story is of a man named Clark. Clark was rock solid in his faith and was as fastidious about his church attendance as he was his dress. He lived his life within strict boundaries of conduct, and expected no less from everyone else. Clark was from a Scottish ancestry and prided himself on his thrifty, almost frugal, attitude towards finances. Clark was a firm steward of his finances, saved, invested and lived a cautious life.—Making do' was an art form for Clark. He was protective of his wife, Alice, and prided himself in her practicality. Clark learned he had terminal cancer in his seventieth year, and accepted the news with a stoic quality typical of his nature. Resisting medical attention when symptoms appeared, by the time of diagnosis, Clarks days were short. Clark was quiet for a few days as the news settled into him. Then he shrugged, and went on with the business of preparing to die. First, Clark told me, he had a long talk with God, saying he wanted to make sure they were OK with each other. Clark told me he was lucky in many ways. He had enough life insurance and savings to feel at peace he was leaving his wife well cared for. He explained to me that coming from the depression generation, it had always been a fear he might not have enough money in an emergency. I understood his frugality better when he spoke of his youth. I could see how his being able to leave Alice well cared for was for him the pinnacle of his life's achievement. Clark spent the next few days taking—care of business' calling his insurance agent, carefully going over the coverage's with his wife by his side. Then he visited the banker and the lawyer, making sure his wife understood Methodically, the two went over the provisions of his carefully drawn will. Clark made sure his wife was informed of all the issues that might arise. Then Clark made his lists: a list about taxes, car insurance and repair, and house maintenance. One by one, Clark turned over the business of their life to his wife. Subtly, but very clearly, he was turning over the power he had held on to for so long. Clark decided he wanted to die at home, desiring as much control over his life as possible he choose Hospice. Clark then seemed to almost to relax, and eased into his death with a rare serenity. Clark said he had done his best with his life, had worked hard, and was now going to enjoy his check out time. Everything was planned and taken care of including his service with readings chosen, the menu he wanted served, who would be his pallbearers, the suit he would wear, and his favorite tie. He had his hospital bed, provided through hospice, placed in the living room in front of the big window in his living room. Clark loved that view and his wish was to die at sunrise. He said he felt that would be a good omen. Good to their word, Hospice was there for him. He had morphine, and knew little pain as he slipped into his passing coma. We who loved him spent the last 24 hours sitting by his side, his favorite music-playing softy in the background accompanying his labored breathing. It seemed to me that before his last breath, just as the sun began to rise, I heard a contented sigh. The rising sun gave Clark his last wish. I believe Clark lived a happy death. He felt he retained control over his life in as many areas as he could. Clark took great satisfaction from his life's work. His wife, while saddened at his passing, felt relief knowing that most decisions were already made for her. Alice gained a sense of control over her life with the knowledge she gained in those last few weeks. Alice also said she now feared her own death less. Clark had given her a road map to follow. "And wasn't that just like Clark"? she asked.

We can learn a great deal from Clark and his careful attention to the world he was to leave behind, as well as from his anticipation of his next adventure, heaven.

Then there is the true story of Chad. Chad was a charming, fun loving man who faced his death in a much different manner. You just had to like Chad. He seemed to behaving a love affair with life, and it was just fun to be around him. I can't remember a time there wasn't a broad grin across his face or a snappy joke coming out of his mouth. Life, he would complain, is something people take way too seriously. A fun dad, loving and affectionate husband, he lived life first class and as a party. His wife, Judy, was his little doll, just as she had been when he married her 50 years before. He would often brag that he took care of everything for her and she never had to worry her pretty little head. Hearing this she would always giggle, saying thank heaven, she could never get by without him. Chad was a generous man. Free with his money for his family, for others, and for himself. Money, he would always say, was to be enjoyed. "Save for a rainy day?" he would laugh, "we live in California, it never rains."

Chad was surprised when it was time for retirement and so little moneys had been saved. Things were pretty tight, still, he laughed, money was not something he was going to worry about. Chad went to church most holidays. Chad said he meant to go more, but he was always so busy. He would joke there was still plenty of time to square things with the—Big Boss'. When he stated feeling tired all the time, it was just an aggravation to Chad and Judy. Soon it could not be ignored, something was wrong. The doctor shocked the two with his grim diagnosis. The party was over. He was sent to the hospital that very day. The smile disappeared from his face, and never returned. His doctor told him that the leukemia would not respond to treatment. "Don't tell my wife that," he snapped, "Don't tell me that". Chad retreated to a private world of anger. Someone had changed all the rules. He stopped speaking to anyone, shutting out even his adoring wife who now resembled a scared, lost kitten. Chad refused to ask for help from anyone, or to plan for a death he feared. God? Well, God had turned his back on him, so he was turning his back on God. It seemed to me that Chad just gave up. He died feeling alone. Even years later, Judy would appear confused, and lost, still waiting for Chad to wake her up and tell her what to do. Chad had lived a wonderful life. He died an angry, hostile and unprepared death. Chad's' and Clark's deaths bring to minds many questions. Are we really helping our loved ones if we give them such a sense of dependency that we leave them crippled in the aftermath? Can we always put off plans for tomorrow? Should we plan for our future financially, as well as for our spirit? Can we afford to wait to discover a relationship with God?

Death should not be life's constant motivation, but we need to give thought to preparation for the day we all know will come. We all learn at a young age, that we are suffering from a terminal condition. As the saying goes, we are never promised the gift of another day. Death often takes us by surprise, just like a rainy day.

I often think of my Mother's death and how profoundly it affected my family. She had Alzheimer's. I watched her disease slowly take her away from us. It is a painful process. I began to grieve for my mother way before she ever died. My Mother had always been one of those who did not like to talk about—serious things'. Talking about death, her wishes, would never have dawned on her even if she had still been herself. But, lost behind the symptoms of the disease, Mother was unaware of her additional problem, lung cancer. She knew she had pain, but from moment to moment, that too would be forgotten. When I took her to the hospital for surgery, I prayed it would be successful, and the pain would stop. My family gathered around her those last five days in the hospital 24 hours a day we were by her side. Her memory was all but gone, but we needed to know we were there for her, for us. She was to die from complications caused by pneumonia. But, before she died, a miracle happened. At least to us, it will always seem to be a miracle. Suddenly, this confused woman became remarkably coherent and a beautiful, peaceful, smile crossed her face, as she described Jesus coming to get her. Those in the room at the time still speak on awe of that moment. Then she fell into a gentle sleep.

It is sad that my Mother left no will, no insurance, no belongings to bequeath, and no parting words. Mother did not actively participate in her death. Still, those who watched it called hers a happy, even enviable, death. Loved ones cared for her, and were with her when she died. Once diagnosed, the pain was masked with medication, so she was not in distress. Her vision of Jesus speaks to her faith and peace at the end. I know it would have really helped us all if we had known of my mother's wishes, and if she had somehow made any plans. Still, I believe in some ways she had done some preparation by her love for her family and her faith. She had planted the seeds that brought forth the fruit of her happy death.

I have learned to believe that part of a happy death is our obligation to prepare ourselves and for our loved ones. I have been repeatedly impressed with the role religion can play in a happy death. In his popular book "Go Gentle Into That Good Night", Malcolm Boyd speaks of the role faith has in life and death. Boyd believes that faith, strengthened with the act of prayer, helps to give strength and peach of mind. To consider the role of death in life without contemplating the role of religion is to many, the same as discussing day without night. For so many of us the biggest question is WHY? Why are we born? Why do we die? We ask big questions. Religion gives us some answers.

Religion gives the believer a promise of peace, and offers to attempt to give an answer to some of life's questions. It tells us God created us with a purpose. If we die, then it is to return to our creator, not to just to become part of the earth. Religion is rich in ritual and meaning. It gives our life substance and hope. Faith, like love, is invisible, but invincible. Faith can make the unbearable, bearable. To face death without faith seems a mission impossible for me. I have seen people die with faith and without faith. Those with faith seemed to have an easier, happier death.

I have tremendous respect for the religious leader, Billy Graham. He believes faith gives us the power to pass through grief, not avoid it. He tells us we are not promised that our faith will erase all fears or concerns regarding ours, or others deaths. But faith is a healer. Repeatedly those questioned have replied that their faith does help. Our faith can be a great comfort. Still, it is OK to need someone to talk to, to cry, to pray, to be angry, to wonder, to questions, and to rant. IT IS OK. THIS DEATH IS YOURS.

4

IN GODS HANDS: TRUSTING IN HIS WORD

Jesus said to his disciples, "Do not let your hearts be troubled. You have faith in God; have faith in me also. In My Fathers House there are many dwelling places. If there were not, would I have told you that I am going to prepare a place for you? And if I go and prepare a place for you, I will come back again and take you to myself, so that where I am I, you may be also be. Where I am going you know the way."

And Thomas said to him, "Master, we do not know where you are going, how can we know the way?"

Then Jesus said to them, "I am the way, and the truth, and the life. No one comes to the Father, except through me." John 14:1-6

The good news is that Christ has given us his promise of eternal life. Part of our goal of reaching a Happy Death is learning to believe and trust this promise. We need to build on it with faith. To have the absolute faith that is required to face death with a calm joy requires us to be childlike and open. By childlike, I am speaking of the open-hearted innocence we wear as a child. It is when we are as a child all things seems possible. As a child, doubt and the trappings of the world do not pollute our minds. We can all remember long ago nights, when as a child we were afraid of the dark. We can remember that calm presence of a parent or loved one, who soothed away our fears. For a moment now, can you turn back in time and remember that emotion? Can you feel the peace and safety return? The dark was still there, the world was the same, but that calming voice of your loved had taken away the fear. This is what our Lord wants to do for us. What he Can do for us.

We will learn in this book a lot that will make your death easier for you, and others. We will learn about medical options, legal matters, funeral planning, about church services, and all manners of things that will help you in your goal for a safe passage. But, friend, nothing will wear as well, do as much, and has a better warranty for that happy death, than your childlike faith.

In Sogyal Rinpochhes book,—The Tibetan Book of the Living and the Dead', he reflects on the importance of religion saying, " Most people, lacking faith in an afterlife, experience a life deprived of meaning. Such a short-term vision results in a brutal world, lacking compassion. At the moment of death the ordinary mind and its delusions die, and in that gap, the boundless sky like nature of our mind is uncovered."

FAITH MATTERS

Having been a Hospice volunteer, as well as someone who has dealt with many other deaths, I can say this from personal experience. People who die with faith, die easier. There is a peace that can be experienced from facing your death, or a loved ones death, with faith. This is a message that will be repeated throughout the book.

St. John Chrsytom questioned, "What, I pray you is dying? Just what it is to put off a garment? For the body is about the soul as a garment. And after laying this aside for a short time, by means of death-we shall resume it again with more splendor."

It really is a sign of passage when we first understand we are born to die. It is assign of faith when we understand we die to live.

It is hard to laugh at the thought of our death, although I believe that—after', we will laugh at ourselves for all our fears. No matter how strong our spiritual growth, we are still living in this material world surrounded by all its needs and concerns. We want to, and should, enjoy this life. God wants us to be happy. HE gave us life to live it fully. Most of us are too busy with the business of living to think much about that vague—no where land' where we no longer walk this earth.

One of my favorite pictures of our Jesus is of him laughing. It is our obligation to appreciate and enjoy this wonderful life. God also gave us our death, so that we may live again with him, eternally Happy in his care. Sometimes it is hard to remember that death is just that instant between you and your meeting your creator face to face. Death and happy, may seem to be words that are in sharp contrast, but they are the sum of Gods promise.

This chapter is to help us remember, and contemplate the promise of our God to help us a shield against our fears. God is not the God of the dead, but of the living: for in him all are alive. In John 11:25-26, Jesus proclaims, " I am the resurrection and the life: those who believe in me, me, though they should die, will come to life; and those who are alive and believe in me will never die."

I just don't know of any insurance policy that could ever offer more security than that. That is a take me to the bank, solid guarantee.

I am fond of the imagery found in Donna Schapes fascinating book,—Stripping Down' The Art of Spiritual Restoration', " God is spreading grace around the world like a five year old spreads peanut butter; thickly, sloppily eager, and if we are in the back shed trying to stay clean, we con't even get a taste."

We need to remember when we are faced with death that the teachings of our faith confidently proclaim that God has created each person for eternal life. We are promised that Jesus, the Son of God, by his death and resurrection, has broken its chains of sin and death. We have the promise from our Lord that when a Christian dies, whose life was begun by the cleansing waters of baptism, and nurtured and fed at the Eucharistic table, that death is not the end. For most Catholics, the thought of death becomes easier because of their acceptance of this theology.

In his book, 'What Catholics Believe', Reverend Lawrence Lovaski remarks, " Life everlasting, as promised in the theology of the church's, as—God made your soul and body for life everlasting, which begins for the soul after death and lasts forever without any change. Life everlasting for the body will begin after the resurrection. The just live forever in heaven. They have died in the state of sanctifying grace, cleansed form all venial sin. They see God face to face and share in his glory and happiness."

Catholics live in the hope of the confident expectation of divine blessing and the beatific vision of God, says the CCC, 2090.

John Paul II has taught, " Life's earthy journey has an end, which, if a person reaches it in friendship with God, coincides with the first moment of eternal bliss. Even if in that passage to heaven, the soul impurities through purgatory, it is already filled with light, certitude and joy, because the person knows he belongs forever to God."

We all live in a time of death and dying. The liveliest of minds and bodies will someday grow weak. The law of dying surrounds everything we do, and think, and feel. BUT, there is also a law of life. That is the law of Christ himself. Christ is the resurrection. We are told by the bible, which is our passbook and guide to this life, that Christ is the everlasting one, resurrected from the dead. HE reaches out to us from the other world. HE feeds our spirit and refreshes our soul. As the old adage goes, you can lead a horse to water, but you can't make him drink. Gods promise for our eternal life is generously offered, but it must be freely accepted.

I can share the good news with you. I can hope that this will rekindle your love for Christ. I can hope it will reawaken your discovery of your life-long process of growing nearer to our Lord. We can say with certainty that for those who die in the Lord, death has power over them only in this world. Death has no power in the next. Your passport gives you safe passage. All the fears, and troubles of our earthly life can follow us there. For the believer, death brings immortal live. While the light of what we know as life goes out, a new, heavenly light is rekindled. Catholic teaching on death is based on the resurrection and says that death is not a final state. The Vatican II taught that God created humans—for a blissful purpose beyond the reach of earthly misery." That sounds pretty good to me.

Rome was not built in a day, nor is a faith that will last a lifetime. We need to water and feed this faith. We need to nurture it and care for it. There are things we can do to help with this process. Read the bible and other inspirational works. Pray, then pray, then pray some more. Allow for some meditative time so you can listen to God talk back. Attend church regularly. Worshipping in the house of God is like the sun with its healing powers. Draw yourself close to those who share your faith, and you will feel stronger by their unity. If, just as many of us who diet are prone to yo-yo, there are times you may weaken. Do not be dismayed. God is THE perfect parent, forgiving and patient. Each day, each moment is a fresh chance to confess, to make new, to forgive others, and to ask for forgiveness. There is an endless supply of water at the well. Come, drink, and believe. Rejoice in this wonderful life. Have faith, accept the promise and indeed, when it is the time, you will find a happy death.

SECTION 2:
DEATH, PREPARING
FOR IT

"SOMEDAY"

And if I go, while you're still here

Know that I still live on

And when you need me, just whisper

My name in your heart,"

Colleen Hitchcock

5

THE GIFT OF LIFE: HOW TO HELP FACE THE HARD DAYS

"Why does the world keep on spinning? Why do the stars shine above, don't they know it's the end of the world, it ended when I lost my love," song lyric from 1960.

LIFE HURTS. In to each of our lives some rain will fall. Sometimes it seems more like a typhoon. We know we should live every moment fully and prepared for whatever life may throw at us just like a good Scout. Matthew 22:13 warns, " Stay awake for you know neither the day nor the hour." Or as my husband Ron always quips, " We are still on the same conveyer belt, and we never know when our number will be up."

As parents we have a driving need to protect and comfort our children. No matter how old they may be, we want to take away their pain. Until I had grown children of my own, I did not understand why she still called me her little girl, no matter what age I was. We never cease to think of our children as our young charges, our responsibility. Parents are quick to love, and quick to forgive. In that, we model our Father. We have such an unconditional love for our children. We wish to spare them hurt. It is hard for us to accept the fact that there are times when all we can do is be there to help pick up the pieces and soothe the tears. We want to feel the pain for them, to spare them .We all have memories of the gentle hand of our parent hugging us and telling us it will be all right. Our Father loves us all with a love so profound we can only begin to appreciate. HE wants us to be comforted. Our Lord loved his Son and had to watch him suffer. Mary watched her Son die on the cross for us. When we pray it is not to someone who is distant, uncaring and unaware of suffering. We are praying to the Master Comforter. We need to remember that no matter how dark the hour, no matter how deep the pain, no matter how overwhelmed we may feel with despair or grief, that We Are Loved. Even at our darkest hour, our faith can take us to the consoling parent who will ease our pain and wipe away the tears.

Still, we may ask if HE loves us why do we have to suffer? That is a big question that has no simple answer. One surely I cannot begin to solve. It is often through suffering that we grow. It is through suffering that we can grow closer to God and understand our Christ. Isak Dinesn in Last Tale said, " It is a good thing to have a great sorrow. Or should human beings allow Christ to have died on the cross for the sake of a toothache?"

Our Jesus Christ gave us a perfect model to follow. His last words on the cross were of acceptance, trust, and faith, " Father into your hands I command my spirit."

No one expects us to be perfect in our faith, but to be growing and striving in our faith. There are times when we will stumble and fall. There will be times when it all seems just too much. I saw this once written on a wall, and it works,—When all else fails, PRAY.'

WHY CAN"T I JUST END IT ALL????????

Because we are human, sometimes a pain can be so overwhelming that we do not know if we can handle it alone. The prospect of a prolonged illness can be so devastating that our spirit sinks. At times that despair can take us a mental place we believed we would never encounter. These can be the darkest of hours. Why we may cry, should we have to suffer so? We may think, why shouldn't I just end this suffering now?

Some of the most controversial issues of our time is the subject of euthanasia, assisted suicide and suicide. This is a difficult issue that we respond to with our own set of moral and religious values. The Catholic Church is very definite on it's stand on this issue .The 1980 Vatican Declaration on Euthanasia defines euthanasia, as "an action or omission which of it self or by intention causes death, in order that suffering may be eliminated".

The Catholic Church teaches that we are not morally obliged to use—extraordinary' means to stay alive, examples being surgery, chemotherapy, ventilator or transplant. HOWEVER, one is bound to do the ordinary; shelter, comfort, feed and water.

In the book—Catholics for Idiots' it is stated, " The capacity of modern technology to ward off death and the failure of individuals, their families, and their caregivers to accept death are factors that contribute to choosing of extraordinary (and often futile) measures. The Catholics Catechism recognizes life as a precious gift and the act of Euthanasia violates the sanctity of life and the sovereignty of

God by assuming ownership of life. The church's teaching affirms the role of healthcare provider as a steward of healing and caring."

Like many of you, I have been touched by the act of suicide. I have seen the painful aftermath that the acts created. We may feel helpless afterwards, but sometimes there are warning signals Often suicide is the last desperate act of an emotionally disturbed mind. It is our obligation to be mindfully aware of the signals that some people send. If we see people drastically change their life style we should be watchful. Have you noticed someone become more withdrawn, begin to give away personal affects, be abnormally sullen or preoccupied with death, sleep more, eat less, any of these behaviors can be a symptom of deep depression.

In dealing with suffering we must remember that in every stage of life, even the painful ones, we have lessons to learn. The last days of an illness can be so difficult, but also bare precious fruit. We can appreciate life with a sharpened vision and taste the richness of every moment. We should appreciate every moment of life God grants us, even the difficult ones at the end. Some may feel, if we are to die anyway why not go now, and end the pain. We need to remember the words of Thomas Aquinas, " When we die is Gods decision not ours."

A good friend of my husband's told him that he does not want to have much medication when he is dying because he wants to fully experience that moment. I feel he is very wise to see the moment of death for the unique bridge that it is.

STILL, WHY MUST I (THEY) SUFFER?

This is such a hard question. We look to our faith for an answer. Watching someone we love in pain and dying painful. When we suffer it is hard to think clearly. It is hard to believe that any merit could be found in that agony. I join with you in the frustration of watching those I love suffer. I know the feeling of helplessness when we have to face suffering with patience, and peace. Yet, I know what the bible tells us about suffering, so I continue to pray and to strive.

In Matthew 10:38, Jesus tells us, " He who does not take up the cross and follow me is not worthy of me". This verse tells us that of part of our discipleship is our willingness to suffer with Him.

John 12:24 says, " Unless a grain of wheat falls into the earth and dies, it remains alone and bears no fruit." Here Jesus is telling us that suffering and death are part of everyday human life. We are told that it is only through suffering and death that we obtain the glory of resurrection.

In Timothy 2; 3:12, Paul instructs Timothy to share in suffering for the Gospel, "Suffering should not be asked for, but it is also not to be avoided."

In Peter14: 1-2, Peter says whoever has suffered in the flesh has ceased from sin to live not by the flesh, but by the will of God. The bible tells as that our suffering furthers our growth in holiness.

Peter says in 1/4:13, "We should rejoice in Christ's sufferings in order to rejoice and be glad when Christ's glory is revealed. Those who suffer with faith in Christ will rejoice in His glory." For as said in 1 Peter 5:10, " After we have suffered, God of all grace will restore, establish, and strengthened us."

If we need to suffer, God promises us that our suffering will ultimately be followed by Glory. This is part of the basic teaching of the Catholic Church. Certainly, the Catholic Church is not saying that it has all the answers to the mystery of suffering. It does have biblical basis for its beliefs. We are told in an encyclical from Pope John Paul II on suffering, " Which reveals God as filled with compassion, freely enduring the suffering of the world. We suffer from weakness, God suffers from fullness of love."

Our greatest remedy for suffering is our faith. The use of the prayer is a powerful tool. Fr. Paul O'Sullivan, O.P. (E.D.M) said, " Suffering is the great problem of human life. We all have to suffer. Sometimes small sorrows, some times greater ones, all to our share. The reason why suffering appears so hard is that, first of all, we are not taught what suffering is. Secondly, we are not taught how to bear it. Thirdly we are not taught the priceless value of suffering".

If we must suffer, then It becomes important to determine what steps we can take for ourselves, and others, to make life manageable at those times we are tested. Some of the answers may be found in hospice, better pain management, and communication with our physicians. Counseling (emotional as well as spiritual), and better use of mental health facilities can offer help and guidance. A great tool is also the opening of our spirit to religious aid. Our lord is waiting for us to ask for his help, for his comfort, and will not leave us alone.

WHERE LAST I LAY MY HEAD
When will we die?

We seek control over our lives but we may not be able to choose the day, hour, nature or location of our death. Few, unless you are on death row and have been given that date and hour, are privy to those last statistics. I, for one, think that is a good thing. Better to be a—good scout' and just be prepared. I think of it like living in California. We all know a major earthquake may happen at anytime. We don't want to think about it. There is no way of knowing when it will happen. We cannot stop it from happening. All we can do is to prepare for that eventuality. I know they will come, so I have bottled water, batteries, and stocked up extra canned goods. I do not live my life each day looking for the ground to move. I am aware that any day, it could. I feel better knowing I have made some plans and have some provisions.

Many of us will learn one day that that we have a terminal illness. We will need to think ahead about where we will spend those last months and days. In this section we will consider some of those options.

First, I would like to proclaim that just as we have a Bill of Rights guaranteed us by our constitution, we are due a Bill of Rights when we are dying:

1. The right to be treated as a living human being until death.

2. The right to maintain a sense of hopefulness, however changing that focus may be.

3. The right to express feelings about one's approaching death in one's own way.

4. The right to participate in decisions concerning ones care.

5. The right to expect continued medical and nursing attention even though " cure" goals must be changed to "comfort" goals.

6. The right to maintain one's individuality and not be judged by personal decisions, which may be contrary to the beliefs of others.

7. The right to be free of pain.

8. The right to have one's questions answered honestly.

9. The right to have help form one's family and for one's family in accepting the death.

10. The right to die with peace and dignity and to not die alone if they wish.

11. The right to discuss and enlarge one's religious and or spiritual experiences whatever they mean to others.

12. The right to expect the sanctity of one's body will be expected after death.

13. The right to be cared for by caring, sensitive, knowledgeable people who will attempt to understand the needs of the dying and be able to gain some satisfaction in helping one to face death.

THE GRACE OF HOSPICE:

Let me introduce you to a wonderful gift. I have learned first hand to have respect for their loving and caring work with the dying. With Hospice, no one need die alone or in pain. Hospice is a palliative, rather than curative method of care. This means that you are accepting that a cure is no longer possible, and that the disease process will end soon (we will die, in other words). The root definition of the word hospice means a community of sojourners along the way, a place for replenishment, refreshment and care.

On our journey to death the gentle, and caring hands of Hospice can be a big component to a happy death. Hospice provides their supportive services to the patients and their families 24 hours a day, 7 days a week both in home and in facility settings. Often when we are dying we fear even more than our death, the thought of pain, of being alone, or loosing our dignity. We fear being a burden to our families. Hospice is aware of those needs and fears and addresses them .The National Hospice organization was formed in 1978. It has become a popular and respected assistant method of care for the terminally ill. Hospice acknowledges that dying is a natural part of living. Hospice does not hasten a person's death, but seeks to give the patient comfort and the best possible quality of life until death. As the saying goes, " We want to live, live, live until we die".

To be qualified for this loving alternative care you need to be suffering from a terminal illness. This can include such diseases as advanced cancer, heart disease, AIDS, lung disease or the complications associated with Alzheimer's. To qualify your life expectancy is to be six months or less. Some of the services that hospice offers includes physical, nursing, medical, therapy, bereavement, dietary, and spiritual care. Hospice strives for its patients to be as alert, comfortable, and capable of enjoying their life and family as possible. With the support of hospice, and its atmosphere of acceptance, the work of preparing to die can be done. And there is work in preparing to die. Beyond all the legal and medical decisions, all the good byes; there is spiritual, and emotional work to be done to be able to meet that big day head on.

I have watched the process and marveled at the gift of grace that hospice workers perform not only for those dying, but also for those who remain behind to grieve. They are such a perfect definition of what Christ asked us to do when he spoke of when he said, " When I was hungry you fed me. When I was thirsty you gave me drink."

The gift of being able to die in your own home surrounded surrounded by a world you are comfortable with, is a blessing. If this is what you choose. One of the big benefits of hospice is the feeling of having some control over your life at a time when we feel we have so little control. I know Hospice will be my choice if I am offered that opportunity. Sometimes we are given notice by illness, and can plan our end, other times it comes more unawares.

6

YOU'VE GOT THE WHOLE WORLD: IN YOUR HANDS UNDERSTANDING YOUR OPTIONS

Choice is a privilege. Choice is a wonderful right that goes hand in hand with responsibility. Choice makes us empowered and feel in control. It gives us freedom. Freedom can give us wings. Choice helps us grow. Until we take our last breath, we are in a continuous process of growth. That is also a challenge

Life, especially as we approach death, often challenges us to make some very difficult decisions (choices). The ever-increasing miracles of modern medicine have caused us to re-evaluate what constitutes life and when to stop the extreme measures. Today there is a complex delicate weaving of science, ethics and religion and philosophy. What is legal may not be what is moral. Some things can be what are called a—social sin'. Modern medicine gives us so many more ways of keeping us alive that dying can become a very prolonged process. Some people near death CHOOSE to allow machines to keep them alive at all costs, while others CHOOSE to bypass heroic efforts, preferring to go at their—natural' time. The question of what is right for you is one of the reasons that having an advance directive is so important. As we talk about directives and Durable Power of attorneys we are facing an important part of your plans for a Happy Death. These tools help to keep you in control. Making your own choices determines that your desires will be followed way, plus it makes it so much easier for your loved ones to know what you want. I was asked to make the decision about life support for my mother. Believe me it is a decision you would prefer the person make for them self. I am sure she would have wanted to spare me that ordeal. Give this issue your serious consideration. Do this for yourself. Do this for your loved ones. Think about it. Pray about it. Decide. Then follow through. Fill out the paper work. The choice is up to you.

PUT IT IN WRITING: A Durable Power of Attorney for Health Care; Your Advanced Directive, allows you to choose someone to state your health care decisions when you cannot. (Who do you feel would best be able to speak for you?) You may choose anyone who is over 18 years of age. In the directive you state your wishes, i.e.: I wish to use all systems available, anything goes, or I would wish to be ventilated, necessitated, food tubes, but do not use extreme measures or limit the measures to include. In an Advanced Care Directive there is no expiration date, unless you have stated a specific time frame. You can cancel or change this Directive at anytime. They are not engraved in stone. You are the boss here. If you do not have an Advanced Directive, your closets relative will be asked to make these decisions for you.

In California there is something called a California Natural Death Act. This tells your doctor you do not want any treatment that only prolongs your dying. It calls for stopping at life sustaining treatment if you are terminally ill, and, a big AND here, if death is imminent.

LIVING WILLS, POWER OF ATTORNEYS AND OTHER RIGHTS

As you make your plans in consideration for others, (as well as out of respect for your own wishes), it is important to deal with the subject of Living Wills, Durable Power of Attorneys, and Your rights to accept or refuse medical treatment. We are always concerned about protecting our rights. What more important area is there to exert your opinion than how you wish to live and die? This is your life, and it will be your death.

ADVANCED DIRECTIVES are documents containing specific information regarding your future medical care and treatment. The two most common directives are known as Living Wills and the appointment of a Health Care Representative. This representative would act in your interests if you were unable to continue to do so. You need to be an aggressive advocate for your medical care and to be well informed. This means feel free, and encouraged to ask questions. You have the right to ask your doctor about all possible methods of care and treatments, their potential benefits and risks. Today there are medical possibilities to extend our life with methods that would have been considered science fiction a few years ago. Like the old limbo game, we may have to decide how low, or how long, we want to go. We have the right to decide if something is beyond what we feel to be realistic life prolonging measures. Cardiac necessitation can bring us back again, and again. Breathing equipment (ventilator) may keep us artificially alive as can a heart pump. There are times WHEN WE HAVE The Right to a choice. Think about whether you would wish to be necessitated or put on those machines. I am not discussing hastening death here; I am taking about artificially extending life. There is no wrong answer here. What maters is making your wishes known so they may be followed. The term for these methods is life sustaining. They are not expected to cure your terminal condition, or to make you better. They simply prolong dying. Examples of these types of machines are the respirator to help you breathe, a kidney dialysis machine to filter wastes, or CPR to restore your heart beat.

WHAT ABOUT THE VENTILATOR? Do you wish to be put on a ventilator? This is one of the decisions you need to make, to have or have not, so to speak. A ventilator is a machine that helps you to breath when you are not able to do so by yourself. There are times when after surgery, or with lung problems a ventilator is used to take over for the body while it recovers. The breathing tube carries the needed oxygen from the ventilator to the patient and the tubes entering the patient's nose or mouth. How long someone may need to stay on a ventilator is dependent on the patients' condition, and may be hours, days, or yes, years.

You may have heard the term Terminal State. That is a condition has been determined to be incurable, that the use of medical treatment will delay, not prevent death. It is when, without these treatments, death would come to you in a short period of time.

Another medical term you may hear is Permanent Unconscious. That state is when you are in a coma, caused by injury, or illness and you remain totally unaware of yourself or surroundings. That condition is determined by your physicians when to, a reasonable certainty, you will not recover.

Your Living Will states whether you would like to have these life sustaining treatments begun or continued. Living Wills are covered by laws that may vary from state to state, so become familiar with your own states laws. While some states call them—directives to physicians', 'simple declaration' or 'declaration' as to medical surgical treatment', the name may be different, but the intent is the same. Relax, and understand that the Living Will would only take affect if you were incapacitated, and terminally ill. Incapacitated would mean when a person is no longer able to understand the choices available to make an informed decision. Most health providers have these forms available. Once you get the form, and think it over, be sure to fill it out. Then return it and file a copy in Your Death Workbook. If you do not like a particular part, scratch it out and initial it. Then sign it before two witnesses. Good for you.

NOW ABOUT THAT HEALTH CARE REPRESENATIVE

Your Durable Power of attorney for health care and health proxy, is someone you will select to make decisions for you when you can't. Every state has it's own limitations, so learn yours. In California there are specific rules as to whom your two witnesses can be; they have to be an adult, cannot be a health care provider or employed of by a health are provider, or be connected with a community care facility, rest home or employee of the above, and also ONE of your witnesses cannot be an heir to any part of your estate. These rules are designed to protect you, and to avoid any possible conflict of interest.

THOSE DO NOT RESECITATE ORDERS are a matter of life and death, yours, and will help tell your healthcare providers what you do, or do not want, done. A do not resuscitate order is a written instruction that a persons doctor places in his patients chart. What this says, basically is, " In an emergency, if the patient heartbeat, and breathing stop because of cardiac arrest, the person does not want to be revived." Discuss with your physician NOW your feelings. There may be some circumstances where you would want to be resuscitated. If you agree to be treated with Hospice a Do Not Resuscitate Order is required. A caveat, in an emergency if 911 is called, in most states emergency personnel will not change their response due to a living will's do not resuscitate order.

7

TIME TO THINK ABOUT THEM; DEATH and CHILDREN

Preparing them to loose. **What if we lose them?**

Thomas Edison said, "When a man dies, if he can pass enthusiasm along to his children, he has left them an estate that is of incalculable value."

Even as I begin to write his chapter, I am overwhelmed with emotion. My mother lioness characteristics are raging forth and I am desperate to think of a way to make this chapter unnecessary. I want to protect my children from everything. They should live forever. It is hard to imagine two more painful and guilt filled emotions than those caused by the death of a child or leaving a child behind. As parents we embrace the roll of caregiver. If we die, no matter what the age of our children, we regret that we will be unable to be there for them. Of course, if we are in the position of loosing young children this is compounded by a multitude of issues and decisions. We will try to deal with some of these in this chapter.

The thought of our children dying, that we are unable to protect them is unbearable. That they may unnaturally go before us is too much to accept. It seems unnatural. It is the pain that has no end. I have many friends who have lost their children prematurely. I have seen the devastating toll that loss takes. We will try to deal with this delicate issue.

Some good news is that many studies have shown that most children who have lost a parent still flourish and live a well-adjusted life after the death of a parent. The main thing to do is to be as open and honest as is age-appropriate with your children about your dying. Children have a built in lie detector machine and they can sense when they are being denied the truth. Their imagination can often create more frightening scenarios than the facts. If you face your death with a calm acceptance and with faith, they will not only be able to handle your death better, but their own death later as well. We are being the guides for them, showing them the path they will someday have to follow. Try to maintain a stable, constant environment as much as possible. Try to maintain regular meal times, for as many of their life's routines to remain unchanged. Routine is comforting for all of us and children benefit from its continuing. Tell your child you are not leaving them because you want to, nor is it because of anything they have done. Tell them that you will always be with them in a special way. Explain to them that love is not seen but remains alive in our heart. Reassure them that they will not be left alone and that others, be it their other parent, family member or guardian will love them and care for them. Often children of terminal parents imagine they also have the illness. They really feel their symptoms. This may be in part from fear they may be dying too, or from their wish to go with you. Reassures them that they are well, and that you are glad that they are well. Tell them it is ok for them to stay behind. Reassure them they are not failing you by staying alive. Children can deal with the topic of differently depending on their ages, and increasing maturity. A young child of say two to seven cannot conceive of death as permanent. A child of 7 through 12 (and, of course, these are all estimates as each and every child is unique, and special in their own right, and matures at their own rate) begins to understand the fact that everyone dies. They know a dead person is not sleeping, and cannot come back. A teenager has an even keener awareness of the subject of death. Most are already struggling with the thought of their own possible demise. It is important to explain to your children that death is a normal process. Tell them death is not a form of punishment, of the one dying or the one left behind. If you have a disease, tell your children. Give it a name, and give them the information you feel they can absorb. Share your faith that you will see them again someday in heaven. Tell them you will wait, but for them not to worry about hurrying. Tell them you wan them to have a long happy life. Let them know you would stay with them if you could. Reassure them your dying has nothing go do with them.

There are many ways we can leave a legacy for our children, beyond the money we invest and contribute through insurance. We can provide more than the legal preparations we make in our wills. These are very important, but we need to leave them a sense of whom we are. The age of video cameras now allows us to make a film of us talking to our children (or grandchildren) at special moments in their future. Another gift we can give is a series of letters to be given at age appropriate times. These can be a real blessing. In a very real way you can be with them at their graduation, their wedding, the birth of their first child. The use of videos can compliment or replace the letters. This is a priceless gift for them, and can be very therapeutic for you as well. Designate in your will gifts you want given at those special times. Have that necklace or watch given to them at a time when its significance will be appreciated. You can plan to create a form of living legacy.

If you talk with your children about death as a natural thing throughout their childhood it will be easier for you, and your child later. Prejudice is for the most part inherited. We often learn it as children from our families. To a great degree, so are our attitudes about death inherited. The gift of our faith to our children is priceless. Our religion, and the bible gives us many tools to use to help with these discussions. Children will pick up on your fears or your faith.

Two big no no's, OK? Do not tell your children death is going to sleep. This is going to make them afraid to go to sleep. It's not sleep, but Returning home to God. Do not tell your child you are going away on along trip, because this sets up a life long phobia whenever anyone leaves for any period of time. Reassure you child that they are healthy and that they will not have to worry about dying for a long time. Time is relative to a child.

THE UNBEARABLE; LOOSING A CHILD

While we may feel we are the only ones to suffer such a loss, millions have shared that loss. Each December there is a World Wide Day set-aside for Bereaved Parents that includes a candlelight Vigil. In my community we have marked out third recognition of that emotional day. Each year the club no one wants to belong to grows larger. At the Vigil parents can bring the pictures of their loved ones and have the opportunity go up to the podium and say, " I am lighting this candle in memory of." All those who participate say they gain strength by the sharing of stories of their beloved child and welcome that opportunity to say their names.

HOW TO DEAL WITH THE FUNERAL

There are special services and rites designed to deal with the death of an infant or child. At times a formal funeral liturgy may be more than the parents can bare and a rite of committal and a prayer may be substituted. Others may need the structure and support that the formal services provide. Funerals may be celebrated for a child who has not yet been baptized. At these services the Christian community entrusts the child to God's all embracing love. The loss and pain connected with the death of a child can be overwhelming. The power of prayer and words from the pastor and others can help the mourner to understand that their child has gone on before them into the Kingdom of God. The funeral helps remind the parent that they will be reunited one d ay with their child. It is helpful for the parents to know they can still pray for their child. Special consideration should be given to the siblings, classmates and friends of the child. If children are allowed to be present at the rite, those with the ability to do so may be asked to participate by reading or presenting a one of the symbolic gifts.

MAKING ALLOWANCES FOR YOUR PETS

For many of us our pets are part of our extended family. They can bring so much joy and comfort to our life. We are their caregivers and because of that they are one of our concerns as we plan for our Happy Death. If you will not have a spouse or immediate family member who will automatically take over your animals care, it is important for you to consider who will be the caregiver for your pet in your absence. A form for adoption of your pet is in your Workbook for that purpose. Be sure and write a list for the new owner telling them of your pets likes and dislikes, habits, and medical history. You may want to make a special contribution in your will for designated for your pets care.

8

THE GIFT OF GIVING

"Don't take your organs to Heaven. Heaven knows we need them here", is a slogan used by a publication speaking of the benefits of donor cards. I know this is a sensitive subject area, and not for everyone. Being an organ donor can lead us to the ultimate way to show our love for our fellowman. Being an organ giver allows you to give the gift of life, love, and hope. Knowing that with our death we will be able to give someone else life, can give our own death added meaning. It can give us a legacy that will live on. It is another form of immortality.

The other night I attended an awards dinner for the American Heart Association. It was a night filled with applause and cheers as we reflected on the recent Heart Walks success. At the closing a video was shown about a young baby born with a damaged heart desperately needing a heart transplant to live. It was impossible not to be moved by the pain of the waiting parents, and the plight of the young baby. Still, the fact that is for this child to live, another must die. The story had bittersweet ending. Another child died, and the transplant was a success. You joined in the pure joy of the one set of parents, while you sensed the others grief. Everyone in the room was touched by the miracle that organ donation made possible.

I have a friend who underwent a heart transplant several years ago. I know the miracle that the transplant has been not only to him, but also to those who know and love him. He has been given the gift of these years and has made each one of them count. I am grateful to that unknown person who, at the moment of dealing with their own loss, chose to give the gift of life.

In the book Catholic Etiquette, it is stated regarding organ donations, " Organ donation is consistent with the churches teaching on charity, as long as the body is handled respectfully. This is an issue we need to decide for ourselves, and then inform our loved ones, to spare them the making of what can be a very difficult decision at such an emotionally trying time. Some people find comfort in the fact that parts of their body can help sustain another 's life."

While the amount of people who are in need of life saving transplants is growing, the available donors are not. While 55 people a day may be saved, 12 people on that same waiting list, die. The Organ Donation Insert Card Act is apart of the Health Insurance Portability and accountability Act (the so called Kennedy/Kassebaum bill) was enacted by the104th Congress to provide donor cards and other information to be inserted into tax returns, starting with refunds made between 2/1 and 6/30/97.

It is understandable that this is a highly emotional issue. It is a question best answered by ourselves after serious consideration. Many fear that somehow they will be denied proper care if they check off that they are an organ donor. Some fear that perhaps eager to get your valuable organ doctors will "let you go". Be relieved, and feel confident that is not the case. YOUR well-being and survival are paramount. You would be considered as a possible donor ONLY if you had no chance for survival. Another prevalent concern is that the person's body will be disfigured and unable to be viewed, this is not true. Your body will be treated with great respect and returned in an acceptable condition for viewing. The cost for the donor harvesting procedure is absorbed by the one receiving the organ and is not a burden to your estate.

Your body has the potential of giving renewed life to 50 individuals. The organs that can be donated include our heart, lungs, liver, kidney, pancreas, and intestines. Tissue transplants can be your eyes, skin, bones, heart valves, tendons, and veins. The human body is a miraculous creation, and the donation of its life saving parts to another of Gods creations is indeed a miracle. Just about everyone can become a potential donor, your age and medical history is not the primary factor. What matters is the condition of the particular organ in need. The National system of the United Network of Organ Sharing works to ensure that organs are matched fairly and with equality. Some of the determining factors are medical urgency blood type, and physical size to create the best match.

There are many organizations nationwide that have valuable information for those interested in being a potential organ donor. A few of them are the Public Education/WWW Project 6464 Dempsey Avenue, Van Nuys, Ca. 91406-6015, Organ Transplant Association P.O. Box 277, Missouri City, TX 77459, The Partnership for Organ Donation, Two Oliver Street, Boston, MA 02109. These are representative of the many organizations that seek to promote a greater public awareness of the worldwide need for increased donation of human Organs, Tissues and Bone Marrow in order to save lives.

SECTION 3:
A GOOD AND LEGAL DEATH

✦

SENSE and CENTS

9

DOING IT RIGHT, AND SETTING IT DOWN

WILLY NILLY: Writing a will is an emotional thing, I know, but the idea of someone else making decisions for me is enough to get me to do it. Are you surprise that 50% of us do not have a will? I just have to many opinions and worked way too hard for my money to allow for someone else to take over. How about you? Dying without a will, in testate, gives some judge, who never met you, to use a cut and dried formula to distribute you money, property and other valuables. And contrary to what you may believe, in many states it will NOT automatically all go to your spouse. Worse yet, if you and your spouse die together, a judge will decide where your children are raised. Is this enough to get you inspired?

You and your spouse will each need your own will. The peace of mind it brings now and the headaches it saves later, makes it worth every penny it costs to have a proper will drawn. We have all worked hard to gather whatever riches we have. Our homes, our investments, these are the lasting material tributes to our life's work. We want to be able to say where they go and to whom, or who for sure we do not want to get them, as the case may be. Don't you want to be the one to say who will care for your children, your business, your parents, your pets? Do you want to have a say in who will make your decisions for you if you can't make them for myself? These are all vital questions and you need to think now about the answers. Have you been in the service, are you a union member? These are important issues. Assume whoever inherits your paper work after you die knows nothing about you. Dot those I's and cross your T's. You are responsible for making an instruction booklet (or will) and instructions and paperwork that is clear and easy to understand. You are not a mind reader, and neither are they, (and you won't be around to fill in the blanks).

WILLS; Will you need to make a will? Perhaps not legally, but if you have wishes and opinions, and who doesn't, how can you not???? You could be in situation where preparing a Will or a Trust is not essential PROVIDED you have arranged a smooth transfer of property. You may have already prepared names, and substitute names in case the first set are deceased, on you r insurance policies. (A Hint: Remember to keep those insurance policies current, and review them with your agent on a regular basis as your needs change. There are so many different types of policies, developed to fit almost any pocket book or situation. Shop around and find one that works for you.) You may have no large or unusual debts that need to be settled. You may feel confident your family will be amiable about the distribution of your wealth, and belongings. (If that is true, you have a very unusual family. Because, unfortunately, the very worst in people seems to come out at these times, often causing life long feuds.) I firmly believe that Wills and the Workbook section will be come a peacemaker as well as insure your wishes. Some time on your part now can settle many long-term family feuds later.

WIL YA HAVE A WILL? Well, a WILL IS a written document that, among other things, designates where your property and assets are to be disbursed. It can also help determine who is the guardian of your children, care taker of your animals, etc. In California, an estate valued at under $60,000 can avoid probate by a process under the Summary Procedure Estate Administration. If your estate is over $60,000 you MAY be faced with a probate of 1 to 1 1/2 years, UNLESS property is titled joint ownership, with right of survivorship (check your stuff now to see how you are listed). This does not involve insurance policies where a beneficiary is stated. Make sure that the person who is currently listed is who you wish to inherit. Many an ex-spouse is rolling over in their grave because of forgetting to do that little thing. If you do not have both names on your cars title, it's not an automatic transfer, check that out. And about that Will, make sure it is properly witnessed, and people know where to find it (use that Workbook).

WHOM DO YOU TRUST? A TRUST is a written document in which you, as grantor, transfer property to a trustee who holds, and manages, the property or assets, for your beneficiary. This can be a long term or limited term Trust, especially if there is a minor child. As we have extended life spans we become more and more a sandwich generation. We care for our children, and later for our parents, facing additional challenges and responsibilities. Trusts can take on any number of shapes, permutations, and restrictions to achieve your desired goals. They can stagger an inheritance over a set period of time.

Your estate is everything you leave behind, be it a mansion, a collection of old baseball cards, a vault of filled with precious jewels or a Tupperware container of pennies. We all have an estate. Your heirs are those who feel they should inherit (your spouse, children, siblings?) or who you wish to inherit, (Your bowling buddy or your barber? Your doggie? Who knows?). Your Will contains your decisions about those very important decisions. Think of it this way, if you go to a restaurant, and you don't look at a menu and order what you want, you will get whatever they want you to have. Even if that means liver and onions, and you hate liver and onions. So do not die with out a Will (in testate).

Now on to TRANSFER of property. I go by the old adage that goes—assume nothing,' because when you assume something it makes an ass out of you and me. You may believe because you are married that your house, time-share, stocks, car, or whatever automatically transfers in ownership to your souse. It ain't necessarily so, so check now. It may mean you need to change some titles or terms on some of your possessions to allow for that smooth transfer later. I have heard of too many instances when spouse's names have not been on bank accounts, safe deposit boxes, stocks and bond among other important documents. A moments time checking now can solve a lot of concern later.

THAT RAINY DAY always come when you least expect it too, and death is like that, too. I suggest you have an emergency fund/death dowry for that very reason. Probate, if needed, can last at least year and other conditions may make it hard for your loved ones to be able to reach your assets immediately after your death. To help your loved ones in this possibility, make sure there is an easily accessible dowry or emergency fund available. This can be a joint checking account (of you do not already have one) or a safe deposit box with shared key. Make sure the other person knows about it, because if not, whoops, it doesn't do much good. This is one of many areas you may want to update periodically as your situation changes, as life with divorce etc. sometimes does.

PAPERWORK, PAPER WORK, RED TAPE, RED TAPE, RED TAPE

What? You thought that all ended when you died? Forget that. Ok, NOW on to Certified Copies of the DEATH CERTIFICATE. Remember the classic scene from The Wizard of OZ when the house fell on the wicked of the East? Now we may have been just watching it on the screen, but we all KNEW she was dead. Still, they had to call out the special coroner to determine that she was not just merely dead, but really most sincerely dead. And certify it, in triplicate!

You need to be determined dead too, house on you or not, and you need the paper work to prove it. That is why you need the certified copies of your death certificate, because every one wants their own proof. The certified Death Certificate is filed with the City or county where the death occurred. While certified transcripts of the death certificate may be ordered at any time, it can be easier to just allow for them in your pre-planning.

Here is a basic list of places that may require copies:

* **Social** security benefits

*Veteran's administration benefits (VA copy provided at no cost)

*Transfer of real property, houses, land, etc.

*Settling of insurance claims (one for each company)

• **Obtaining union benefits**

•**Transfer of automobiles, trailer,** boat, camper (DMV)

* Transfer of stocks and bonds (one for each company)

• Transfer of bank savings or trust accounts, and entry into safety deposit boxes,

• Filing of Federal or State income tax

• Insured loan or insured credit card accounts

• For Credit Union Accounts

• Mortgage Insurance

• If there is an estate to settle, your attorney

• Pension Plans

WHAT SHOULD YOU HAVE IN YOUR PERSONAL PAPER SECTION:

1. **Your** birth certificate, and if possible, copies of your spouse and children's birth certificates.

2. **A copy of you r social security card.**

3. Marriage certificates, and if applicable, copy of divorce or annulments documents.

4. A copy of your Will and Trusts.

5. A copy of your Living Will or advanced directive.

6. Copies of mortgages and titles to properties

7. Life Insurance policies.

8. . Statement of Union Benefits

9. If you were in service, that documentation.

10. A copy of your preplanning agreement with your funeral home, including copy of your plot, if purchased from cemetery or agreement with Cremation Charter.

11. Filled out information sheets in Workbook of contacts and policies.

10

WHAT YOU DECREE

There are many ways we can control our life. There are some ways we can control what happens after our death. This section has been designed to help you feel that control, and to take advantage of where you can make a difference and make your wishes known.

One way to do this is to create an Executive Cabinet. If you are married, this is one of the nicest things you can do for your spouse. The creation of the forms on Your Death Workbook combined with your funeral preplanning are a wonderful resource for your loved ones. The Cabinet you create is an on going treasure that they will bless you for many times over. Knowing that they exist will make you rest better. These people will be your representatives in their areas of expertise, after you are gone. Honored as most are to be asked for such a title, be sure and check with these people first before you place their name in your Cabinet. These people would include, but not be limited to: Your attorney for advice on legal matters, your insurance agent for insurance advice, your real estate agent, accountant and tax advisor, your favorite banking representative, your stock broker or investment counselor are all ones you might think of, and are very valuable. Remember to list the electrician you really trust, the plumber, the painter, carpenter, landscape person, travel agent, and other crafts people you may have been the only one to deal with. Then we get down to the personal advisors. These should be people you know and trust that you believe would give the same caring, loving, and fair advice you would if you were still there. If your spouse has decisions to make about the children, her ill parents, should she move, does the house need the roof or should she just sell, is it ok for her travel yet, what, why, when and how??? A list of people you trust could be a real asset.

SECTION 4:
HAVING IT YOUR WAY

❖

BEING THE DESIGNER OF
OUR DESTINY

11

YOUR LAST FAREWELL

◆

ONE FROM COLUMN B

We are now going to deal with your final farewell, that last big party, your bon voyage; your funeral. Oh, I know it takes a lot of courage, maybe even a good stiff (pardon the pun) drink to think about these kinds of plans. So if you are not exactly dying to do this (sorry, there I go again), read on and come back later. This is a really important chapter. I know you have your likes and dislikes about other funerals. I know you have opinions. Really, how can you not want to have the last word here? So many decisions and choices, and no one knows you quite like, well you. If you have some general shopping information you will feel more like an informed consumer. So here goes, take a deep breath.

A TISKET, A CASKET

The world is filled with variety. Variety is the spice of life. Believe me there are a world of choices in the world of final bedchambers, other wise known as caskets. They say build a better mousetrap and the world will rush to your door. We are forever trying to reinvent ourselves and our customs. The American is the ultimate entrepreneur. And that does not stop at the business of death, which is a multi-billion-dollar business. A good example of this sense of the entrepreneur was depicted in a Peoples Magazine article of November 02 about Casket Furniture, (I'm dead serious). Mark Zeabin's unique handcrafted casket/furniture are the ultimate of versatility taking you from a coffee table in life to your slumber chamber in the after life. A wood worker, he began making coffins in 1997 after his grandmother's death and discovering that the cheapest burial box at his local funeral home cost more than $1000. His creative juices working, he began to carve beautiful, bargain caskets for no more than $295. Zeabin regretted that his beautiful craftsmanship was 'deep sixed' so soon, and so the transitional casket as furniture was born

Caskets now are designed to fit almost any mood from Egyptian sarcophagus's to looking like a golf cart or have Elvis painted on the top. You can go as fashionable or avant-garde as you wish. Tombstones come in many shapes and designs and offer you many ways to have your last word. You can be buried, in ground or in a mausoleum or be cremated offering you an assortment of even how you get to exit. There is big business in dying, and a lot to think about. First let's think about which way that you may want to be buried.

IN GROUND BURIAL: You need to know about this if you are considering a traditional burial. A burial vault is the outside container into which the casket is placed. It is designed to protect the casket and keep the grave surface from sinking in. Burial vaults vary, they can be built of one or more of these materials; concrete, stainless steel, galvanized steel, copper, bronze, plastic and fiberglass.

MAUSELUEMS: A thumb nail sketch for you of the alternative to ground burial, the mausoleum, tells us that the first mausoleum was built back in 353 B.C. by King Mauslus (hence the name, Scripture tells us that Joseph of Arimathea went to Pilate and asked for the body of Christ, " He then took it down, wrapped it in a shroud and put him in a tomb which was hewn in stone in which no one had yet been laid (Luke 23:52-54)"

Throughout the church's history, mausoleum—style entombment has been utilized. Our early Christians were buried in the catacombs. Private mausoleums can be found in some older cemeteries, but because of their costs were usually available only to the rich. Today prices are more affordable and for cemeteries that have these facilities they can be a real option to below ground burials.

Ok, we are thinking about a crypt, what is involved?

The crypt

The entombment fee

Memorial Plaque with Inscription

Vase for Flowers and Future Care of the Facility

It some cases it can cost more in ground burial than it odes for crypt entombment, depending on grave selection, memorialization and the concrete outer burial selected for the casket.

Another term we will deal with when planning for our funeral is Embalming. Depending on where you live and your circumstances, embalming can be a matter of choice. Your decision will be influenced by the length of time between death and burial, enhancement of deceased appearance in an open casket for public or private viewing, and transportation of body by plane or train.

SO, IT'S YOUR PARTY AND YOU'LL DIE IF YOU WANT TO

This is about planning your last party. Maybe you have let others plan your wedding or birthday parties, or cruises or getaways, but THIS really is your last outing, so HAVE IT YOUR WAY. These are really big decisions. They are easier made in the calm of life by YOU, than later on during a time of great emotion and stress by someone else. Planning your funeral is a great gift from you to your family and friends. It spares them wondering what you want, and all that worry. And who knows what you want better than you? Think of all the Christmas gifts you have returned over the years, the horrible ties and sweaters, the vases you've received that made you say. " What on earth were they thinking?" I keep thinking about the white casket with the pink roses I was shown when I made my plans. Talk about not my style! It would have killed me to be buried in that one, not that it wasn't pretty. It was. It just was not me. Did you ever see the television program—Providence?' I loved it. Anyway, the Mother on the show dies in the first episode wearing a green dress to her daughters wedding (she has a heart attack from the stress of planning the wedding, which is understandable enough) and dies during the ceremony. Talk about ruining a perfectly good wedding. Since that episode the mother reappears in dreams to one of the daughters in every show, still wearing, you guessed it, the same green dress. For five seasons this poor dead Mom was in fashion limbo. In several episodes she laments that she wished she had taken better care when she had dressed that last morning, moaning. "If only I had known this would be what I would wear for eternity." Actually, on the last show she got to graduate out of limbo and wear red, but that is another story. So, wouldn't you like to specify what you'll wear that would SUIT (and tie or not) you. I know I would come back from the grave if you put me in a pastel dress. My husbands Mother, whom I loved dearly, had a special blue dress stuck aside in a cleaners bag at all times. I am not THAT good, but I have made suggestions n my notes. Pencil in a few ideas of your own in your workbook.

The cost of a funeral can really kill your budget. So planning ahead, and becoming a savvy shopper is smart. And later on everyone will say that, too. It is sort of like how my Mother always warned me to always wear clean underwear in case I was in a car accident. We usually have no idea when we are going to die. So you'll rest easier now, and then, if you have these decisions well made, and well behind you. I say, prepare for your death. Then forget about it, and get down to some serious living. Come on you know you shop and compare cars and detergents, why not funeral home services? Sadly, a few funeral directors count on the fact your family will be upset and make emotional not wise financial decisions.

Your loved ones may be made to believe they can best express their love by large tickets choices. Now if you want the biggest and the best, by all means go for it. But, try to choose it yourself or at least say in your instructions you want to go out like first class ala Trump. If you pride yourself on being practical, preplanning is good sense for the money it saves. It also saves worry, tears and the fears for your loved ones. I really do understand, that some of you cannot do this. I know that the thought of pre-planning scares you to, well, about scares you to death. Or, you really would rater die than, ok. But please, at least write some of your ideas down in your workbook to help others make those decisions for you.

We can bee motivated in many ways when we plan another's funeral.

I think of a story I know about a woman who had not loved her husband. She had married him very much on the rebound. When he died, her guilt was overwhelming and she decided she could make up for her past discretions by giving him the biggest, most expensive funeral. She felt that somehow a lifetime of behavior could be erased by an extravagant last gesture. Then she heard of a young couple that was very in love, but in great need. She remembered how her deceased husband had always been a hopeless romantic. Now she was ashamed how she had ridiculed his affection for weakness. This caused her to see a way to make a real tribute to her husband, not by a gesture of wealth, but by a gesture of love. After much prayerful thought, she chose to have the funeral be simpler, and decided to help the couple instead with the extra funds. Her heart lightened with this decision. She felt that she had made a better a tribute to her husband's memory by encouraging love and life.

Then there is the true story of how a son's cheapness in planning his socialite mothers' funeral triggered the talk that eventually led to an official investigation, and his conviction for her murders in Tyler, Texas. The wealthy deceased had been a very extravagant woman. When her son gave her a very simple funeral with only one small flower spray on the cheap casket, tongues wagged. How much could he have loved his mother, they asked, if that was how he sent her off? Just think, had his mother planned her own funeral, he may have gotten away with her murder.

Another story I know is of a young man. Though only in his twenties, he was very old for his age. He seemed to carry a burden and had a heavy sense of responsibility. He had lost several friends and worried about how his possible death would affect his single mother. At an age when few think of life insurance, he went and got a policy to cover his possible funeral costs plus, he smiled, just a little extra. He visited a funeral home, made his simple plans, and wrote his mother a letter. He seemed to feel so much better with that business, as he referred to it, out of the way. Perhaps he had a sense of premonition, for he was killed in a car accident just a year later. The mother could not believe that she had nothing to do. Her son had it all arranged, and the insurance covered it all, plus a little more. In the letter he left his mother, he left her instructions of how that money could help her with a new life. It was amazing. His legacy of love to his mother never left her. .

SO, what is for you?

We need to think about a lot of issues here and we will deal with them one by one.

Do you want a funeral, or memorial? Burial or cremation? Wake or reception? Graveyard services? Flowers sent or donations to a favorite charity? Music and prayer or a drink at the neighborhood bar for everyone? A funeral that people, will talk about the rest of their lives, by which all other funerals will be measured, or a quiet, simple affair with just family? At the beach or in the church? Do you want a Rosary? Or do you want to be ashes scattered and speak of me no more?

We are each unique, and so are our wishes. One of my daughter's has a fantasy funeral where every guy she ever dated is present and they are all uncontrollably weeping. The image makes her smile. Joking side, she has decided she wants to be an organ donor, and then be cremated with her ashes scattered on a location she calls Heavens Highest Hill. My husband Ron has images of horse drawn carriages, black plumed horses, with a swaying Dixie band following his hearse with a Mahalia Jackson type singing while others wail. He also wants to be sure that everyone we owe money to is there so they can cry they'll never be paid. We all have our dream weddings. Some of us have our dream funerals. It is hard to think about guest lists, food selections, and musical choices for a party you will not attend, but since they are all going to talk about you when you're gone, you may as well give them something good to say.

Funerals are a formality that for many is steeped in tradition. They often are a combination of the deceased personality, family traditions, nationality and religion. As we will discuss in another section, the Catholic funeral is rich with ritual and tradition. The sense of formality and historical continuity can be very comforting.

ONE FROM COLUMN B

If you choose to be buried, then it is time for the case of the consumer right casket. How much should we spend, what type do we want, what about lining? There are more types of casket choices, various materials and linings than choices at Subway for your sandwich. From simple pine at basically bargain prices to the ultimate in luxury, the sky really is the limit for this groundbreaking purchase. As emotional an issue your funeral is for you and your loved ones, funerals are also big business. There are big bucks for others to be made in our dying, with over 25,000 funeral homes in the United States handling millions of dollars annually.

There are several major categories of services that we will need to deal with in our discussion of savvy service shopping. California law requires services to be listed item by item, and you are free to pick and choose, just like at your favorite Chinese restaurant.

Professional services includes the viewing or slumber room where your family and guest can go sit with you and reflect .You may or may not choose to have people visit or come pay respects, list this on your plans. While you are considering this, think of whether you would want a closed or open casket at these viewings. There are nor right nor wrong answers to these questions. No one is going to pop out of a Miss Manners Book and tell you that its wrong funeral etiquette. These are your wishes. Even the use of a Funeral Home (FH) for your ceremony or memorial service again is an OPTION. You may choose to use a funeral home just for their prep care and have your service at your a church or synagogue. If a cremation is in your future you may use very limited services, especially if you belong to a Cremation Membership. (Cremation will be discussed later) You may choose to have just a memorial service at a time after your actual burial or cremation to allow for their loved ones to come to grips with their death or be able to travel and attend. Some may make special recommendations that if their death is near a specific holiday (Christmas for instance) that a service or memorial beheld at a later date out of consideration of family members. I have attended Memorials held months after a loved ones death.

You may or may not wish to have graveside services. Some feel the closure involved in attending a service graveside to be helpful; it may even be part of their religious or national heritage. We have all been to funerals where loved ones place a rose on the casket before it is lowered or who drop hands full of dirt, as part of the closing ceremonies. In the Catholic Church it is ritual to have the grave blessed, but this does not mean there needs to be a regular service held graveside.

Personally, I have chosen to have no services at the cemetery, (but will have my grave blessed.) I believe that it only prolongs the grief and that the image of lowering a coffin in the ground is a lasting one. However, I have spoken to many people who say that to the contrary, the image of the lowering of the casket helped them with their closure process.

I DON'T HAVE A THING TO WEAR; or what do you want to be caught dead in? Even if you are going to be cremated, you may want to decide what you should wear for your last outing. So, put your ideas in your workbook. If not something specific, say a dark suit and tie, or one of favorite dresses I wear to church, or anything blue.

If you do not want to make any of those type of decisions or have anything from your closet go with you (maybe you always hated all of it anyway) you may be surprised that many funeral homes have a section where they sell clothes, including peignoir sets, really). Do you wish to wear any specific jewelry such as your class ring, your fathers watch, your sorority tack, your masons ring, the broach Aunt Ida gave you or your favorite pearl stud earrings? Say it now. Wedding rings can be a particularly hot issue. Are they until death do us part or are they going the whole nine yards with you? Many people want to leave their wedding rings to their children, so if that is your choice be sure and have that stated in your plans and with your information at the funeral home. My wedding ring will go with me; the rest of my jewelry will be divided between my girls.

MIRROR, MIRROR IT'S A CURSE,
FOR MY LAST VIEWING
DON'T HAVE ME LOOK MY WORSE

Or, coming face to face with death and not being able to do a thing with your hair, when you really don't want to have a bad hair day. I've got to quote Edgar Frienberb who wrote in his book, The Vanishing Adolescent, "No American is prepared to attend his own funeral with out the services of a highly skilled cosmetician. It is part of the American Dream to live long and die young."

I still remember the terrible blue frosted eye shadow that was on my beloved grandfathers eyelids at his funeral from over fifty years ago. The look is far more natural now. I am a great fan of HBO's landmark series Six Feet Under, about a funeral home and have been fascinated by the scenes, which depict the cosmetic genius at work. If you do not plan on being viewed, another of your many decisions (I do not want to be viewed) say so, and that eliminates this concern, but if you have a particular wish or concern, mark that down.

Hair raising stories aside, do you want your hair up, down, with that favorite barrette? Have them make sure the roots don't show? My beloved friend and hairdresser, Lou Vierra, tells me she will do mine (as is a custom, I am told, for most cosmeticians to serve their clients that one last time, just think you won't have to tip).

To some of us the idea of how we look or what we where may seem unimportant, to others it is a vital issue. Two television shows come to mind. The first is about a young mother who is dying who had always read her son a story about magical dancing shoes. The son becomes determined to get his dying mom a special pair of dancing shoes so she can look her best when she goes to heaven and is able to dance. It is an extraordinary, ten hankie movie. It touched in so many levels the need for those we leave behind to feel they can comfort us as we leave. The son found the special shoes and his loving act did give him a sense of peace. On an episode of the popular television series of The District, the main character, a Chief of Police, is at the death bed of a young woman who dying of Aids. While he sings her a sweet version of Amazing Grace he is painting her toenails a bright red. She had explained she needed her toes painted so she would look pretty when she first saw Jesus. His was an act of love, and a very tangible a way he could comfort her. Her request was a sign of faith. She was certain she would be seeing her Jesus soon.

Now to back to some, ahum,—ground breaking' basics:

VAULTS AND LINERS are another cost to be considered with burial costs. A liner is a metal or concrete shell that the casket is lowered into to prevent moisture from getting into the grave and deteriorating the grave.

THE OPTION OF MAUSELEUMS: Our local cemetery has a lovely mausoleum that provides a serene atmosphere to allow you to visit your loved one, and meditate in climatic comfort. Its stained glass windows are beautiful and it gives me a good, calm feeling to be there. Others tell me they feel it is cold and dreary, and they would prefer to be out in the sun. That is why Baskin-Robbins boasts having 31 flavors. We all don't love vanilla.

The price range, as with caskets and plots, vary in prices from about $3000 up and up. They do have some saving graces when you consider the costs you loose with a mausoleum in lieu of burial, such as the opening and closing of the grave ($500 up), no vault liner ($500 up), or Monument ($650 up), and no plot ($500 up). There is a charge for the marker. Many mausoleums allow you to display a picture of your loved one (or yourself). Another benefit of mausoleums is there are not the same concerns of moisture, grave collapse or damage to the casket.

The book, The Affordable Funeral, Going in Style, Not in Debt", by R.E. Markin is filled with e research on this and other topics dealing with the financial end of funeral planning. I encourage readers to check it out. It is always wise to be an informed consumer.

GOING TO THE CHAPEL AND YOU"RE GOING TO GET BURIED; TRANSPORTATION TO SERVICES

Grabbing a taxi won't do, but just what are your options and costs? Transportation services provided by the funeral home of your choice can include the transfer of the body in a hearse, limousine to transport family members and flowers transported by van. It is not mandatory to rent a limousine for transportation of family, but many prefer to have that service as a convenience as one thing they do not have to worry about. Often a friend or family member will offer to drive instead. You may want to include a limousine as a gesture to your loved ones. If included in your plans, it can be a sign of appreciation for them for their presence at your service. The important thing to remember is that you do not have to have a limousine.

MERCHANDISE

YOUR LAST SHELTER: The types of caskets available for you to chose from are as varied as you can possibly imagine. A rule of thumb is that generally the cost of your casket is about 15% of the cost of the funeral. Let's consider a few of the more common types; Steel caskets are graded by gauge from 8 to 26, and are considered to be the most reasonable end of the metal casket lines, comprising about three fourths of all caskets sold. The Copper, and bronze caskets are more expensive and are graded by weight, usually 32 to 48 ounces. Wooden caskets are still popular and appreciated for their craftsmanship and are made of mahogany, walnut, cherry, maple, poplar and pine. These can run from pressed particle bard with cloth linings to works of art lined with rich satin. Hard wood caskets account for about 15% of all caskets sold.

SERVICE: CASH ADVANCE ITEMS

This category of expenses can include an Honorarium for Clergy, flowers, newspaper notices, soloist, and death certificates (remember typically 12 are needed), air transportation, cremation permits, crematory charges, acknowledgment cards, burial plots and perpetual care for cemetery, as well as monument or marker expense.

These items come with a lot of decisions and potentially a great deal of expense. What matters most to you? Maybe your family has a plot back East and all that matters to you is for you to be flown back there. Then make that plan and follow it. Many families have found out too late (after burial) that there was a family plot somewhere. That has caused many a family feud. Yes, some family members DID suggest that the body be dug up.

CREMATION

Cremation has been around for all of recorded history. It is rich in the history of ancient Australians, Babylonians and Greece. Cremation did not begin to fall out of favor until the modern civilizations of the 17th and 18th centuries. It is now having a great upsurge in popularity. Certainly direct cremation is one of the least expensive ways of disposing of a body. You don't need to have it embalmed and you have the option of using a low cost container. The ashes can be placed in a cardboard box or plastic container and given to your family.

IS CREMATION FOR YOU?

In a recent television episode of Whoopi, the main character played by Whoopi Goldberg tells her brother she wants to be cremated when she dies. When he asks her why, she replies, holding her cigarette in her hand, " Because then I can have one last smoke. Then afterwards spread my ashes around in the best ash trays in town."

Way before cremation was a good punch line, it was steeped in ancient history

Cremation has been around for just about forever. Rich in history, it fell out of fashion in the 17th and 18th centuries. It has become an increasingly popular choice over the last few decades both for economic and geographic reasons. Boy, is this an issue that people have—heated' emotions about, it is either for you, or it ain't. We will try to look at it from several points of view to help you make your decision.

This is a big decision because it can erase a whole set of other issues. . Like many questionnaires you see where is says if not applicable go on to line whatever. The section on casket and liners and all the assorted goodies is only relevant if you choose ground burial or mausoleum without cremation. So, I give you permission to skip the sections that do not apply to you just like in those wonderful questionnaires we all love so much.

The Neptune Society is a Cremation Service with several locations through out California. They feel they offer a real alternative to traditional funeral ser ices. They are among a growing number of businesses in the world of death services to encourage pre-planning and pre-payment. For their Registration service for Pre-planning they charge a nominal fee of $25 for your arrangements be placed on file. This enables—member' to pay a lifetime charge that relieves the family and loved ones of planning, but not the involved costs. If you choose the Pre Planning method that fee is waived. A real benefit of Pre Paying they say is that the costs involved with the cremation and scattering of ashes are frozen. Funds for this are held in a refundable trust and monthly payment plans are available. Sort of a pay as you die plan.

The Neptune Society says they were founded to provide an alternative to the costly and involved process of traditional funeral arrangements. They tell me that they are devoted to the simple and dignified disposition of the decedents remains. The services of the Society includes removing the body from its last resting place, placing it in a container, holding the body in a refrigerated facility, the preparation of all legal required paperwork, dealing with family for arrangements, the cremation (this usually takes place 5 to 7 days after death), the memorial service (if requested), and the storage of ashes until dispensation.

Want to have an idea of how much? Your wish is my command.

ESTIMATE OF SERVICES

Basic Professional services $455

Transportation (includes removal of body) $350

Car and Driver for filing $95

Cremation Container (before tax) $45

Cremation and Refrigeration $395

Total Basic Cremation Cost $1340

DISPOSITIONS

Deliver to Sea $100

Garden Scatter (in a designated local cemeteries) $100'Sheet Bronze Urn (others are available) $25 Processing and Handling of Placement of urn $75.

They also offer memorial services with chapel (up to 40) $295, Minister $100 to $250, folders up to 75 at $25, memorial books $25, viewing f one hour $125, dressing $75 and preparation of autopsied remains $125. Feel like a savvy consumer about? If you are looking for a bargain, cremation is certainly your most economical option.

CREMATION AND THE CHURCH

The Catholic Church's attitude on cremation has changed greatly over the years. We need to remember that the tradition of burying the body goes way back before Christian times. For centuries cremation was forbidden by the church because of the belief that the body is the temple of the Holy Spirit, as well our belief in the resurrection of the body. Cremation was seen then as a pagan practice that denied the doctrine of the Resurrection. The long-standing ban against cremation was lifted in 1963. Up until June of 1996, however, the container with the ashes was not allowed in the church. The Vatican eliminated that clause in March of 1997 when they said that they granted permission for the created remains of a body to be brought into the church of a liturgical rite. It is still, however, the churches preference to have the full compliment of funeral rites take place with the body present and have the cremation afterwards.

When cremation follows the liturgy, embalming is usually necessary. When cremation follows soon after death, embalming is not necessary. Each state has its own regulations, but the general ruler is that the deceased human body, which is not buried with in 24 to 48 hours, is to be embalmed or refrigerated. However, simple embalming and the use of a cremation casket need not be an expensive consideration. If you choose to have the body present at the Mass, many funeral directors offer caskets for rent, as well as the special cremation or shell casket that you may purchase.

Burial options for the remains include a family grave in a cemetery marked with a traditional memorial stone, or in an urn garden, a special section in a cemetery with small, pre-dug graves for urns or a columbarium. A columbarium is an arrangement of niches, either in a mausoleum, a room or wall in which an urn or other vessel is placed for permanent memorial. I am told that niches generally range in price from $400 to $1400.

The Church does not believe in the scattering of ashes due to the belief that the remains of the body should be treated with the same respect given the human body from which they came. It is the opinion that the scattering of ashes deprives loved ones and descendants of the opportunity to visit the remains, where they can pray and reflect. The exception is burial at sea. An appropriate and worthy container, heavy enough to be sent to its final resting place, may be dropped into the sea. The burial of cremated remains at sea in this manner seems to be an appropriate alternative to the long-standing custom of a traditional sea burial.

One last thought on Cremation. I was recently watching a made for television movie on HBO called—Behind the Red Door' which dealt with great sensitivity the death of a man from Aids and his relationship with his sister during this passage. Throughout the film the image of drawn red hearts are used. When the man decides on cremation, and after his death, a striking fact is revealed. It seems that the temperature at which a body is cremated is not determined by the degree at which the body will burn. The heart, made of muscle will not burn at that temperature. The degree of heat used to cremate a body is determined by the heart.

12

A PLAN IN THE HAND

✦

IT'S A GOOD THING

Let me share with you an unusual, but very productive day. Like many of you, I have a tendency to put thing off. For all my good intentions (after all I am writing my second book on dying) I had failed to do one of their most basic recommendations, gone to the funeral home of my choice and actually put it down in writing (and with a check to boot). I felt very grown up when I left, and very relieved. I was glad that it had been me that answered those guest ions and not one of my bereaved (I am going out on a limb here and assuming my family members will be a little upset). The funeral director of our local Funeral Home, the ultimate Day's End Hotel, informed me that about 30% of his funerals now have been pre-planned. This speaks to the growing trend of our wanting to have it all OUR WAY, as well as a real sign of love for those we leave behind.

The whole process of planning my service took less than an hour. It really was painless. The gal who was my—travel guide' was pleasant, and very understanding. She was a little thrown by my casual attitude toward my death arrangements. Most people, she smiled demurely, were a little more—sober' about their being there. "Why is that?" I asked with a surprised look on my face, " I thought people were dying to get in here." I explained that I had given the process great deal of thought and was just here to—formalize the deal'. She said it helped her a lot to know I had already given some of these questions consideration. My suggestion to you is that while you read this chapter you think about what some of your responses might be. They will be needed for your workbook at the end of the book. You or your loved ones will need them when those final departure arrangements are made.

I told her I had already purchased my plots at the neighborhood cemetery, and I planned on a casket burial. This cut out asset of questions you might deal with, if you need to purchase plots, a space in a mausoleum, or if you choose to be cremated. I want you to feel familiar with the wide variety and types of burial, caskets materials, and other options, so you will be a savvy shopper. Hearing of my purchase, the assistant called the cemetery to give me their other costs, these fees include the opening and closing of the grave, and I was quoted $1285. I told them I wanted a Rosary at their Chapel ($250) and a Mass at my church ($250). They explained to me some charges. First there is the cost of transfer of remains to mortuary ($175) with second attendant (additional$ 50), and if I am thoughtless enough to die after hours, well that is an added cost ($145) There is a basic professional service fee of $1146, (now remember these are figures I was given, different Homes in different areas will vary, but it gives you a thumb nail budget) Then there are the costs of embalming (required because I am not being cremated of $250 and then a dressing, casketing and cosmetic fee of $175.) I have asked for a closed casket and she made a notation, but the charge is the same. The charge for their Graveyard services is an additional $250. I tell her I do not want graveyard services, but for the services to end at the church. I request just to have the priest bless my grave, and she makes that notation. Then we add the vehicle cost of the hearse (for me, $175, hope it's a pretty one for that)) utility van (if anyone sends me flowers, $60), and a pallbearer limousine ($35, the least I could do). Now we are on to merchandise. Boy, caskets can go from next to nothing to, well really something and the prices range right along with them. The sky is the limit, so to speak. Then I was taken back into the Slumber Shopping Room. I had a wide variety to choose from, plus catalogs galore. I have fairly simple tastes. I told her I wanted something in good taste, but understated. I chose a black metal job with angels on the ends, for $1765. I chose to purchase the Memorial package ($75) of little pamphlets they give out at the funeral because I know I like to keep them when I attend a funeral and place them in my bible. So I thought maybe some of the visitors at my service may want to do the same. If not, I give them permission to make paper airplanes out of them. I made a special request that I wanted to write the poem for the inside, which I did and it is in my folder at their office.

This is the poem that I wrote:

> "What is it that makes us so fear death
> When all it does is take our breath
> And transforms the warmth that fills our heart,
> Simply to another part
> Where we fight no more with sword

But touch the hand of our lord
I trust the promise my lord has made
Do not worry, I am not afraid."

See, I always have to have the last word.

Sentimentality aside, now on to other charges. I chose to purchase a double headstone ($715). Our cemetery only allows us to have flat markers so that limited me on my choices. Become aware of the limitations of your cemetery or shop around if you live in a city with more than one cemetery. I chose a double marker because I want to be buried next to my husband. I was able to tell them what I wanted written on the stone, and she made me a sample right there and then. The wonders of computer programs never cease to a maze me. Then there is the cost for Certified Death Certificates (I estimated that I would need 12 at $10 each that is $140). I explained who you may need those copies for in another chapter. Then there is the charge for the coroner ($100), and the courier fees for $65, if those services are needed. Additional charges included were for the clergy's services for $100 and for music (I chose a vocalist who charges $125) SO my basic funeral bill looked like this:

Basic Professional Services Fee	$1146
Transfer of remains to mortuary	$175
Second attendant, if needed	$50
After Hours, if needed	$145
Embalming	$250
Dressing, casketing, cosmetics	$175
Visitation/Rosary	$250
Church Service	$250
Use of hearse	$175
Utility Van	$60
Pallbearer Limousine	$35
Casket, black w/blue lining	$1765
Memorial Package	$75
Marker/double flat	$715

Merchandise tax	$185
Burial permits (12)	$140
Clergy honorarium	$100
Musician	$125
Coroner's fee/if needed	$100
Courier/if needed	$65
Cemetery fees	$1285
—Total estimated cost—	$7266.24

THEN, I was asked to fill out a Memorial Guide Form to be kept where someone knows it is but NOT in your safe deposit box. I like the wording of the introduction, which read:

To My Family, It has been my wish to spare you worry, anxiety, and expense in the event of my death. Below are suggestions to guide you in making my final arrangements, together with vital information that you will be required to complete the necessary legal records. I respectfully request hat these suggestions be considered as closely as possible in completing my final arrangements.

VITAL STATISTICS
Full name
Address   City   state   zip
Birthplace/ city/ state   Date of birth
Telephone number
Name of Spouse
Fathers Name   Birth place
Mothers Name   Birthplace
Social security number   Citizen?
Occupation   Employed   Employer
Years residence established in county   state

MILITARY RECORD
Name of war   serial #
Date and place of induction
Date and place of discharge
Insurance policies in effect
I have/have not made a last will and testament
It is located at

FUNERAL SRVICE REQUESTS
Name of mortuary   city /state
Place of service chapel   / church
Church Denomination
Pastor
Lodge Participation   Name of Lodge

Person to make final arrangements
Address/phone
Special requests
INTERNMENT REQUESTS
I prefer earth burial cremation mausoleum
Name of cemetery   city   and state
I have or have not reserved facilities
Signature and date
OK, Feeling good?? Simple and easy. Don't worry copies of all these lists are
in your Workbook.

—Send Me No Flowers' was the name of a very popular old Rock Hudson
and Doris Day movies, but is it how you feel? A popular add on television advises
us to say it with flowers. Many people choose to do just that when a person dies.
Some people count the love or respect a deceased receives by how many arrangements arrive, and that is to bad. Flowers are a lovely way of sending a tribute but
there are many other ways, often of more lasting value. Put your thoughts on this
subject in your planning sheet in the Workbook. Do you want flowers? (I love
yellow roses) Do you have any preferences, any ideas? Perhaps you would like to
make a notation that whatever flowers you receive are delivered to a favorite hospital or convalescent home for others to enjoy. Maybe you would like to request
that in lieu of flowers they send a donation to one of your favorite charities. This
is what I want, so put that down. People are not mind readers, and it is especially
hard for our loved ones to read our minds after we are gone. Just for kicks (I have
a strange way of getting my kicks, I know), I went on line to check on the price of
some funeral flower arrangements one store had a lovely standing cross made of
fresh roses for $179, another boasted of their floor basket arrangement suitable to
be sent from family for $129, while another described a floral heart for $175.
Obviously with funeral flowers the skies (or heaven) are the limit.

13

HAVING THE LAST WORD

◆

LEAVING YOUR MARK AND HAVING YOUR SAY

Having the last word is important to most of us. In a very real way our epitaphs, and eulogies are our last chance to get in that last word. In this chapter we will discuss these opportunities, and I hope they will stimulate you to get you motivated.

I remember playing a game once when we had to describe ourselves in just a few words, and you know what, it was hard. Imagine how hard it us for our loved ones to think of a few words to summarize our life? Some people simply do better others under emotional pressure, and having given several eulogies myself, believe me, it is pressure. While a very great and sincere honor, there is a sense of tremendous responsibility in the task of memorializing the life of a loved one. We want so much to express the sense of the person, to serve them well. It is because this part of your funeral service is so important that I encourage you to choose several names for your plan sheet. By selecting several names that you feel good about, it makes it easier for your family to number one not to have to decide themselves and to know they are following your wishes.

We will begin this section with one of the oldest customs around, the Epitaph's

AND THEY'LL ALL TALK ABOUT US WHEN WERE GONE…

Our Epitaph (as in let no man write my epitaph, I would rather write it myself, thanks)

"I will have the last word, in stone no less.

I want those words about me to express me best

So for that epitaph, if indeed I got to go,

I want to be the one to tell you so."

Epitaphs go way back, even back in the days of the pyramids, engraving one's last thoughts was not only fashionable, it was big business. Think of the hieroglyphics (talk about being long winded, those Egyptians were not shy about singing their own praises) the engraving, the huge stone testimonies to the life of the deceased. Pharaohs made sure no one would ever forget them. They created a form of massive rock immortality. Indeed, one of the first forms of written self-expression is the tombstone epitaph. These blending of statistical fact, and emotional declarations are the engraved culmination of a lifetime. When we walk through cemeteries and read the engraved messages we are given a glimpse into the hearts and lives of those who have gone on before us. Our loved ones will return to our markers and read them for generations. Those few engraved words will be testimony to our existence long after we have gone on to our—better things.'

I must admit, I have always been drawn to cemeteries. I have read many markers, and wondered about the lives they represented. I have been fascinated thinking of how we were more alike, than different. We were both, after all, in the cemetery. Only, for now, I was visiting and they were occupants. They already knew the answers to so many of my questions, and none of them were talking. The only hints they gave me were on their markers.

For your enjoyment and to create a flow of creative juices to help you pencil in what you might want on yours, I am sharing some of my favorite inscriptions from tombstones.

Here lie the remains of H. P. Nichol's wife
Who mourned away her natural life,
She mourned herself to death for her man
While he was in the service of Uncle Sam (died 1863)

Death is not an eternal sleep,
Therefore my friends you need not weep:
But look by faith beyond the grave,
That you some peace of soul may save. (Died 1802)

I am with Christ, which is far better"(died 1880)

Been here and been there. And had a good time (died 1859)
Two of my favorites are anonymous quips, "O reader be prepared " and this comes from 1790" Reader pass on and ne're waste your time, On bad biography

and bitter rhyme, For I am this cumbrous clay unsure, and what I was, is no affair of yours."

Perhaps there is something you would especially like to be remembered for like, Carlisle Graham who died in 1868 boasted on his tombstone, " First to go through the Whirlpool Rapids in a barrel and live."

One of the more famous epitaphs of our time is on the marker of humorist Dorothy Parker. Parker passed on to life's next chapter with her tongue in cheek request, "Excuse my dust".

Few of us are that witty or that succinct. So what would you want your stone to say? How would you have your name engraved? A woman may wish to have her maiden name as well as her married name or names as the case may be. Zsa Zsa Gabor, and Elizabeth Taylor might have a lot to think about. Some may want just want one name like CHER or Twiggy. Maybe you want your middle name engraved, while others would rather die)(bad pun) than for you to find it out. My Fathers middle name was Engelbert, and he did not want that out (whoops!) My middle name is Diane, but I go by Diana. So I will have my name Diana Joyce Ingram). I am from out of state, but love California and will be buried here. Some of you may be particularly found of being from New York or Texas, or wherever. That may be something you would want on your stone. Maybe it is being a mother, grandparent, doctor, teacher, painter, golf enthusiast, a Rotarians, Portuguese, that you associate yourself. What words would you use to define yourself? For a fun exercise list twenty-five words to describe you and use them as a place to work from. Some of mine would be wife, mother, grandmother, pet lover, Catholic, writer, dreamer, and optimist.

My stone is already designed and in my file at the funeral home. It is a double marker. I have followed my own advice and already purchased our connected plots (with the perpetual care paid for because I always have a hardener and I don't want the neighbors' to talk about me.) While we plan to have our names Ron (not Ronald) and Diana Joyce Ingram, we wish to add the line—Ronnie and Joycie Together Forever,' making a statement on our devotion to each other. WE are Ronnie and Joycie to each other, and would not let a little thing like death come between us. Now when you find that place in your workbook for your epitaph, maybe it will have more meaning for you. Leave 'em laughing, leave 'em sighing, leave 'em crying, but do it with your own words.

MARK THESE WORDS: Now what about the slate those words are written on? That leads us to the subject of markers or memorial stones. To determine the cost and type of marker that will bear those well-chosen words, first you need to find out what your chosen cemetery allows as markers. Many cemeteries now have limitations. As I mentioned before my local cemetery now has only allows flat surfaces monuments. As to price, the sky can be the limit. The most commonly used material is granite, which comes lighter, least expensive to the more costly, but better quality medium and darker shades expensive. While marble is popular with some it can have problems with oxidizing and discoloring sooner. Research shows that you can—usually' get better bargain (besides a larger selection) at a monument dealer than at a cemetery

While we are still talking about words, how about your eulogy?

AND SPEAKING OF DOTTIE: ME, MYSELF AND I. THE EULOGY

IF you are planning on having a memorial service, vigil the night before the funeral, and in some funeral masses, you may wish to include in your plans a Eulogy. This is the time when someone goes to the front and tries to give a brief, usually very emotional, tribute to, or summation of your life. It is a time for people to say how much you have affected their, and others life's. Wouldn't you just love to be a fly on the wall for that? It would be the ultimate ease drop, huh? While we may not be able to do that, we can think about whom we would like to give it. It might be a good time to consider that, now. As we mature and out lives change, we may go back and change our funeral plans numerous times. That is just fine. It is healthy to review your choices from time to time, just as it wise to look over your will, and other arrangements so that they best reflect YOUR wishes and needs. Make a pencil list of about five people as possible candidates that if you were to die now, you would like to deliver your eulogy. Some of you may wish your family members to deliver your eulogy, but do you believe they will feel up to the task? I have delivered several eulogies for friends, and it is was an honor. I was unable to deliver my Mothers. I wrote it, however, and gave it to someone else to read. I know of several friends who knew they were dying who wrote their own eulogies as a form of farewell letters to their loved ones. They were read out loud by an appointed friend at their service and they were especially moving. It seemed as if a part of them was in the chapel with us, as of course there was. Perhaps you may want to write a few thoughts down as a guideline for your workbook, or perhaps you might want to say NO Eulogy. This is your farewell sendoff, You are the boss.

14

FOR THE VALIANT; VETERANS RIGHTS

If you are one of the dedicated Americans who service our country, this section is for you. If not, consider yourself given permission to skip a chapter.

The rich heritage of being in the service provides for the veteran some resources for burial, IF they wish to use them. President Abraham Lincoln established the original National Cemetery system in 1862. Its' goal at the time was to provide for the registration, and burial of the thousands of soldiers who lost their life during the Civil War. Since those early beginnings the system has gown to expand to over 114 cemeteries in over 38 states and Puerto Rico, as well as 33 soldier lots and memorial sights. The population of new tenants at these cemeteries is expected to continue to grow as we deal with the group known affectionate as the Baby Boomers. Many of our National Cemeteries are already filled to capacity for—casket' burials. * Cremated burials are still accepted at most sites. Spouses and children of veterans already buried at a National cemetery are allowed to be buried with them per conditions of burial. New sites for additional National cemeteries are being given consideration.

One gravesite is allocated for each eligible member, assigned at time of need. The burial plot, opening of the burial site, closing of grave and perpetual care, and a government marker is provided at no cost. The costs of additional head stone inscriptions are not included, as well as the cost of serves provided by the funeral director, and related expenses incurred by next of kin. Your funeral arrangements are to be made by your nearest relative or your acting representative in association with your selected Funeral Director. Then they should provide the Veterans Cemetery Director with the copy of your signed discharge papers, or the veterans name, rank, serial number, social security number, VA Claim number, birth, and death dates. The cemetery will then verify eligibility so interment can take place.

Military honors are not automatically provided by the National Cemetery. However, the cemetery will provide for your representative a list of military contacts for them. The list of honors may include uniformed body bearers, rifle salute, a bugler playing taps (one of the most touching things you will ever hear), chaplain, and a folding flag detail.

I have attended many veteran funerals, including my Uncle Glen Day's. They are a beautiful, poignant ceremony that will leave a lasting memory for your loved ones. They are filled with the reverence and respect you or your loved one deserves. .

There is normally one headstone provided for each family member within one grave. For years the standard was an upright marble stone, but in recent years the flat insert stone is more commonly used. Check with your local National Cemetery to find out their particular standards. The headstones are provided by the U.S. Government (free of charge.) Nice to get something for free even if you have to die to do it) to mark the unmarked grave of eligible Veterans in any country. Memorial headstones are available for eligible veterans whose remains are not recovered, are buried at sea or donated to science. Niche markers are available for those who are cremated. Medal of Honor headstones are available for the graves of such recipients. Headstones must be engraved with the name, branch of service, years of birth and death, and in that specific order. Your next of kin, or representative, must apply for the headstone/marker using a VA form when a burial is to take place in a private cemetery.

Because viewing facilities are not available at National Cemeteries this services (if wanted) need to be arranged by your funeral director. Normally formal committal services are held at a separate location from the cemetery. Internment takes place after that service.

SECTION 5:
DEATH THE PROMISE

"Yea, though I walk through the valley of the shadow of death, I will fear no evil for thou art with me"
OUR ULTIMATE LIFE INSURANCE POLICY

15

THE PROMISE RESURRCTION AND HEAVEN

"He that believeth in me, though he were dead, yet shall he live, and who so ever liveth and believeth in me shall never die." John 11; 25-26

Those who read the bible know that it is rich in its promise's to the faithful. We are repeatedly reassured that Heavenly glory is the destiny that Our God intends for us. The reader is consoled with the news that God wants us to know eternal bliss and peace and joy. We are promised by our church doctrine that death is indeed not the end, but a beginning. We are promised that Death is but a rite of passage to eternal life, our return Home for our reunion with God. WE are promised that He cares about each and every one of us. We are promised that each of our life's and death's is, " Precious in the eyes of the Lord is the death if his faithful ones."(Psalm 116:25)

Our promises are legion; John 14:1-4 tells us, " I solemnly assure you, an hour is coming, has indeed come, when the dead shall hear the voice of the Son of God, and those who have heeded it shall live."

Once more John consoles us with this promise, " Do not let your heart be troubled.

Have faith in God and faith in me. In my Father's House there are many dwelling places otherwise, how could I have told you that I was going to prepare a place for you? I am indeed going to prepare a place for you, and then I shall come back to take you with me, that where I am you also may be. You know the way that leads where I go."

The Catechisms of the Catholic Church describes heaven as " The ultimate end and fulfillment of the deepest human longings, the state of supreme, definite happiness"(1024).

St. Paul wrote, " Eye has not seen, nor ear heard, nor the heart of man conceived, what God has prepared for those who love him."(I Corinthians 2:9)

The church confidently proclaims that God created each person for eternal life, and that Jesus, the Son of God, by his death and resurrection has broken the bonds of death. I liken life and death to the periods of Advent and Christmas. With the period of Advent we are in a stage of anticipation and preparation, waiting for the birth of our savior. Then we celebrate with great joy upon the recognition of his birth. In many ways our life is a period of preparation, and anticipation for our reunion with our creator. Our death, and arrival in heaven is likened to Christmas with the gift of eternal life.

We can live our lives alone, or we can live our lives with faith. God gave us Free Will and that means we choose. With Christ we need never be alone. HE would not have us die alone. We must trust in his word. When I find myself caught up in the fears and concerns of daily life I try to remember the scripture from Matthew 6:28, "Consider the lilies of the field, how they grow, the neither toil nor spin, yet I tell you, even Solomon in al his glory was never closed lie one of these."

If God gives such radiant loving to his flowers, can I expect he will not lovingly care as well for me?

Bishop Seen once remarked, " Shall we place our joys in time or eternity? For we cannot have them both. Shall we mourn before we die or after we die? For we cannot have both. We cannot have our reward both in heaven and on earth."

I remember hearing the old saying, " Eat drink, and be merry for tomorrow we may die." The message seems to be that we better grab life with gusto, for later we are going to be really hungry. A popular bumper sticker warns us SHIT HAPPENS AND THEN WE DIE. Geese Louise!! Do you buy that??? We have this wonderful, creative God, who makes this complicated, yet remarkably balanced world, and He would have it be for nothing???? I believe HE wants us to enjoy our time on earth. I really do. I also believe that The Trinity wants us to respect our body, the Earth, and each other, as the temples they are of HIS work. BUT, I do not think this is all there is, nor do I believe that THIS is the best.—After' is the dessert. Yes, I do believe there is a light at the end of the tunnel of life. I believe that it is brighter and more wonderful than we can even begin to imagine within our minds limitations.

Think of the gift of Easter and the Resurrection for all its many layers. Yes, we are given the gift of forgiveness for our sins. Yes, for those who believe we are given the promise of eternal life. Do you believe that? In Luke, when the women go to Jesus tomb and discover the stone rolled away they encounter two angels.

One of the angels asks this haunting question, " Why do you seek the living among the dead? He is not here, he has been raised."

What is our lesson here?

TRANSFORMATION COMES FROM THE RESURRECTION: When we die, we do not remain in that shell we have outgrown. Just as a butterfly leaves behind its cocoon when it takes flight in its improved, more beautiful and free state, we are transformed. If a butterfly tries to leave his cocoon prematurely he will not be develop fully. The butterfly will not be able to go on to its next stage of development. So it is with us. We cannot choose the moment we are ready for that transformation. When it is our time, we will be taken.

This is really the nitty gritty of the death issue. Our attitude towards death is pivotal on our belief or non-belief of the afterlife promised by the gift of Jesus Christ. It is like thinking you would have to go through labor forever and never have the baby, if you do not believe. It is mixing the ingredients for a cake in the bowl and spilling it and not letting it bake to a golden brown and turn into a wonderful cake. As night follows day, death follows life and with faith, life follows death. Death with faith is the shot that makes you get all better. It can give us such peace now to learn to believe and TRUST in the promise of the resurrection. FAITH can make death a detail to arrange, something to plan for but not with dread and fear, but to approach with hopeful anticipation. It can be Bon Voyage, I am going home!!!

TIP TOEING THROUGH PURGATORY

This can be a touchy subject, but it is a crucial part of our faith.

For most Catholics, there is the belief that some voyagers may make a few stopovers after their death before they can have their joyous arrival in heaven. In the amusing and informative book,—Why Do Catholics Genuflect and Answers to Other Puzzling Questions About the Catholic Church,' Al Kresta speaks of the church's belief in purgatory, " The catechism of the Catholic Church limits its discussion of purgatory to four paragraphs, in them it is said 'All who die in Gods grace and friendship, but still imperfectly purified, are indeed assured of their eternal salvation: but after death they undergo purification, so as to achieve the holiness necessary to enter the joy of haven'. Purgatory is that temporary state or place, condition or process after death by which we are in Christ are purged of disordered self love and cleansed of remaining moral and spiritual imperfection."

Wow! That is a lot to comprehend, so let's go further. John Paul II has taught that, " Life's earthly journey has an end which, if a person reaches it in friendship with God, coincides with the first moment of eternal bliss. Even if in that passage to heaven, the soul must undergo the purification of the last impurities through purgatory, he is already filled with light, certitude and joy, because the person knows that he belongs forever to God."

I know that is what I hope will be my final destination. If it happens I need to have a lay over, well I am ready to do what ever it takes to gain that final entry. And, I will take all the prayers of intercession I can get, thank you very much. Candles, masses, prayers, I am sure I can use any I can get. All will be very appreciated, thank you very much. One of the unique attributes of the Catholic Church is our belief that we can pray for others in that fashion. This belief that we are a united family of God, and that we can offer prayers up gives added character, provides value and richness to our funeral services. This process allows those who grieve to be able to take an active part, to do part of the Work of the Word. Our church tradition rich services not only comfort the living and honor the dead, they help send on those cleansing prayers. I like that.

I like this passage on purgatory found in the words of St, Catherine of Genoa from 1447–1510, " No happiness can be found worthy to be compared with that of the soul in purgatory except that with one of the saints in paradise (heaven). And day-by-day this happiness grows as God flows into their souls, more and more as the hindrance to his entrance is consumed. Sin's rust is the hindrance, and the fire burns the rust away so that more and more of the soul opens itself up to the divine inflowing."

Sometimes when we are on vacation, heading towards some beautiful paradise we can't wait to get to, we run upon a detour. That detour may make it take a little longer to get to our desire destination, but the goal is to get there. I cannot imagine anything more desirable than being with our Lord. Whatever work it takes, it's worth it.

16

THE LAST BLESSING;
THE SERVICE

◆

HOW IT'S DONE AND WHY WE DO
THE THINGS WE DO

Our faith is such a gift. Faith pays the best dividend of any investment I know. Our prayers are well repaid. With us as a garment from birth to death, our faith will travel with us through the good times and the bad. As we draw to the end of our voyage on earth, our faith is a particular blessing.

The Catholic Church has a long, and rich history of guiding people to prepare spiritually for their death, and for assisting with the illness and death of loved ones. Let's consider its formula.

Three separate, and sequential rites are proposed as the most fitting way to celebrate the pilgrimage of the deceased Christian. The three, the Holy number of the Trinity is fitting in the three days it took for our Christ to a rise. The Eucharist helps to heal the sorrow that comes from the loss of a loved one. The Church service allows us to celebrate, offer worship and praise and thanksgiving for the gift of the life returned to God. The service affirms the Church's belief in the sacredness of the human body and the resurrection of the dead. It helps to commend to the dead to God's merciful love and to plead for forgiveness of their sins. It helps to bring hope and consolation to the living. The service helps to renew our awareness of God's mercy and judgment and to meet the human need to turn to God in times of crisis and need. The services help to support the churches emphasis on the indispensable role of the world community in the dying and the death if a Christian. Our services and rites help to affirm and express the union of the church on earth with the church in heaven in the one great communion of saints. We find that the celebration of the funeral rites actually helps to promote a healthy grieving process that can lead to spiritual growth. The Catholic tradition urges the church today to face death with honest rituals that preserve Christian and human values. We are reminded that it was through Christ the victory over death was won.

Cardinal Maida of the Detroit Diocese says that, " Perhaps more than any other moment in the life journey, the time of death and dying is a premier opportunity to come to know the abiding and healing presence of the Risen Lord in, with and through his body the church."

We are blessed when Christians celebrate the funeral rite to offer worship, praise and thanksgiving to God for the gift of life which as been returned to God. The Mass is the memorial of Christ's death and resurrection. It is the principle celebration of the Catholic funeral. It feeds the soul, nourishing our spiritual needs, and provides us with renewed strength and hope for our united future.

A Church funeral does so much for the comforting of the loved ones, as well as for the deceased.

THE RECIPE

As when we are baking a cake that requires a certain combination of eggs, sugar, flour, water and other ingredients to make a successful dessert, there is a recipe for a Funeral Mass.

Lets think about some of the ingredients.

VIGIL: This may be at the church, home or funeral home or be represented by the recitation of the Rosary the night before the Funeral Liturgy. After the Prayer of Intercession and after the blessing, is the appropriate time during the Vigil for a friend or loved one to speak of the deceased.

PSALMS: These are readings from the bible that are rich in feeling and imagery. They help express feelings of suffering, pain, and other human emotions in a passionate way that people can easily relate to.

HOMILY: This is a brief talk based on scripture readings, not a Eulogy, that should concentrate on Gods compassionate love. This helps to give comfort and inspiration to the loved ones at the service.

INTERCESSIONS: These are carefully chosen texts that capture unspoken prayers and hopes.

SYMBOLS: The Easter candle helps to remind us of Christian's victory over death. During the funerals liturgy as well as during the Vigil service the Easter candle may be placed near the coffin as a sign of reverence and solemnity. It is a sign of our trust and hope for our resurrection to life everlasting.

HOLY WATER is used in the rite of the final commendation as a gesture of blessing and farewell.

INCENSE is used during the Rite as a sign of honor to the body of the deceased, as well as a sign of the community's prayers for the deceased.

PALLS, depending on customs, a Pall may be placed over the coffin when it is received at the church. It is used as a reflection of the baptismal garment of the deceased. His is an elective symbol.

PRESENATION OF GIFTS

Your Bible, or a Book of Gospels may be presented during the presentation of the gifts and placed on your casket as assign you lived by the Christian word. I was honored to carry the Bible of a dear friend of mine at his Funeral Mass and placed it on his casket. It was a very significant moment to me. It provided a feeling of being involved in his service that will never leave me. This may be something you wish to include in your plans. If so, be sure to designate whom you wish to carry that very important symbol for you.

A Crucifix may be placed on your casket as a sign of Christ's suffering and his victory over death. This is another opportunity to include a significant person in your service and to choose an item of significance to you personally in your service. I have seen many examples of this and it is very moving. I have a crucifix that was presented to me by my beloved Monsignor and I wish to have my friend Lou, who is also well as my original church sponsor, to place it on my casket. At a recent funeral I was attending the internment service at the local cemetery. Once more I watched the touching custom of placing crucifixes on the casket, the priests sprinkling the casket, and the crosses. The reverently he presented one to each of the immediate family member to take home as a permanent expression of the promise of the resurrection. That action, as it always does, affected me deeply. It is a perfect example of how symbols and ritual can be used to help with the grieving process. Many Catholics wish to be buried with their favorite Rosary in their hands, and I am no exception. If you have this wish, note it in your funeral plans, and be sure and specify which Rosary (that is if you are like me and have a real collection).

FLOWERS may be placed on your casket, usually from a spouse or child or someone with close connection with the deceased, and are used in moderation.

Note at Catholic funerals only Christian symbols may be used to rest on or near the coffin. Items such as flags would need to be removed before entering the church.

THE PROCESSION, especially when accompanied by music and singing can strengthen the bond of community in assembly. During various processions, it is preferable that the pallbearers carry the coffin as assign of reverence and respect. The Procession constitutes the heritage of Christian Rome which consisted of three stages or stations joined by two processions, Christians accompanied the body on its last journey from the home of the deceased the Christian community proceeded to the church singing psalms.

THE LAST RITES

These used to be known as Extreme Unction. This is the sacrament when, through the anointing with blessed oil by the priest, and his prayer, gives strength to the soul and sometimes body, when a person is in danger of, or near of death. What does this sacrament give? It provides the pardon of venial sins, and mortal sins. If you have at least, imperfect contrition (your soul is clean), it provides comfort and peace and the promise of eternal life, and gives the pardon of at least some of your temporal punishment. Only a priest can give extreme unction. In case of sudden death a priest should always be called. The church believes that absolution and extreme unction may still helps for sometime after a person appears to be dead. It should be remembered that a person can ask for this anointing of the sick for a variety of reasons, including going into surgery.

PALL Bearer: At large funerals usually 6-10 mourners are asked to be chosen as pallbearers. Who would you choose? There is a section for those names in your Workbook. Pallbearers may be Honorary. In this case funeral home staff does the actual carrying of the casket. Traditionally pallbearers have been men, but etiquette says now that women may be asked to serve in that capacity as well. Non-Catholics as well as Catholics may be pallbearers at a Catholic funeral. Normally (now remember this is your funeral) dark colored clothing is worn by the pallbearers. They usually sit together towards the front of the church, and arrive a little early. Friends or relatives may be asked to serve as ushers as well.

MEMORIAL SERVICE: The traditional difference between a funeral and a memorial service is the body. A memorial is often held for one lost at seas, died in a distant country, or was cremated. There has been an increase in the amount of Memorials over the past few years because of time, distance, flexibility and expenses. It is also common for a funeral to be held for the deceased where they die, and for a memorial to be held at a distant location to accommodate family members out of state.

THE PROCESS: A new development for many churches is the bereavement committee, which helps to involve the family with the planning of the Funeral Mass. The family is able to work with the bereavement committee to choose the selections of the hymns, psalms, and readings to be used. This is an area where your Workbook sheets come in handy for your family, as you have all the work done for them

LITURGICAL COLORS: These colors chosen for the funeral should express Christian hope, but not be offensive to human sorrow. In the United States white, violet, or black vestments may be used.

FORMULA: There are three main Ritual moments in the Catholic funeral; the Vigil with related rites and prayers, the Funeral liturgy and the Rite of Committal.

Lets look over a basic funeral service format:

Introductory Rite; This includes the Greeting, Sprinkling with holy water, optional funeral pall, entrance procession, optional placing of Christian symbols, and opening prayer.

Liturgy of the Word: These include Readings from the bible, responsorial psalm, Gospel, Homily, and General Intercession

Liturgy of the Eucharist

Final Commendation: This includes the invitation to prayer, moment of Silence, sign or a song of farewell, and prayer of Commendation.

Procession to Place of Committal

Rite of Committal: This includes the Invitation, scripture verse, prayer over place of committal, committal, intercessions, Lords Prayer, Concluding Prayer, and Prayer over people.

AFTER THOUGHTS

When Buddha was asked how many people used their lives fully, he scratched the earth with his fingernail, and pointing to the dust he had picked up under the nail, replied, " This many as compared to the weight of the world."

Life is not a dress rehearsal is a line my children heard so many times they could recite it in their sleep. The poignant scenes from the play—Our Town' depict the pain of realizing too late, the joys of life we overlooked while we were here to enjoy them. Heaven, I have no doubt is well just heavenly. I hope that this book will help you face that final victory with peace and planning. But, God does not make junk; in us or in the world he created for us to protect and to enjoy. Each and every day is filed with so many beautiful sights, smells, sounds, sensations and opportunities. We can never drink enough from the well. Life is a never-ending source of pleasures and chances to live fully and to live well. Our souls are capable of giving endless love; pure and ample it is waiting for us to share. Love recreates itself just like the bread and fish of that memorable meal Jesus fed to the masses. We will not run out of laughter, it will grow back ten fold, so why do we hoard them it along with all those unspent smiles, unused giggles and hugs? Why do we feel we have only so much love to give, only so many ways to share, so many talents to use? Why do we hold things in we are meant to share?

The Lord made the world and it was good. We are meant to enjoy it. We are meant to be good to it, and each other. God gave us life and it is good. Breathe in deeply. Feel the wonder of the world our God created and gave to us. Let us be happy. And then, when the time comes, with faith in our God, we will be happy in death as well.

YOUR DEATH WORKBOOK

PUTTING YOUR THOUGHTS IN PRINT

I HAVE ALWAYS WANTED TO GO OR DO:

YOUR DEATH WORKBOOK
YOUR GOOD BYE LETTERS

Person	Address	Reason

MY FACTS

Your Name _____

Street Address _____

Birth date _____

Place of Birth _____

Social Security Number _____

Military ID _____

Retirement Date _____

Marriages/Spouse _____

Birth date _____

Place of Birth _____

Date of Divorce _____ Place _____

Date of Death _____ Place _____

Place for additional spouse if needed

PARENTS:

Father _____

Street Address _____

Phone _____

Birthplace and Date _____

Date of Death _____ Place _____

Mother _____

Street Address _____

Phone _____

Birthplace and Date _____

Date of Death _____ Place _____

CHILDREN:

Name _____

Street Address _____

Phone _____

Birth Place and Date _____

Social Security Number _____

CHILDREN:

Name _____

Street Address _____

Phone _____

Birth Place and Date _____

Social Security Number _____

REFERENCE ONE

IN AN EMERGENCY CALL:

Doctor's Name _____

Street Address _____

City, State, Zip _____

Phone _____

Ambulance or Rescue Service _____

Street Address _____

City, State, Zip _____

Phone _____

FIRST TO CALL: Relative or Friend

Name _____

Street Address _____

City, State, Zip _____

Phone _____

Back-up Choice _____

Street Address _____

City, State, Zip _____

Phone _____

Clergyman or Spiritual Advisor _____

Church/Denomination _____

Street Address _____

City, State, Zip _____

Phone _____

Funeral Director or Cremation Society _____

Name _____

Funeral Home _____

Street Address _____

City, State, Zip _____

Phone _____

Attorney Name _____

Street Address _____

City, State, Zip
Phone

LOCATION OF FAMILY RECORDS

Birth Certificates: _____

Self _____

Spouse _____

Children _____

Adoption Papers _____

Naturalization Papers _____

Passports _____

Marriage Certificates _____

Divorce Certificates _____

Death Certificates _____

Medical Information _____

LOCATION OF IMPORTANT PAPERS

WILL _____ Dated _____

Location _____

Executor _____

Phone _____

Attorney _____

Address _____

Phone _____

TRUST _____ Dated _____

Location _____

Trustees Name _____

Address _____

Phone _____

Purpose of Trust _____

INCOME TAX RECORDS

Prepares Name _____

Tax Year _____ Phone _____

Location of Files _____

EMERGENCY FUND

Bank or other _____

Address _____

Phone _____

Account Number or Safe Deposit Number _____

CREDIT UNION/BANK/SAVINGS AND LOAN

Institution Name	Account Number	Address	Phone

Location of:

Checks _____

Passbooks _____

Statements _____

Canceled Checks _____

LIFE INSURANCE

Company _____

Agent _____

Address _____

Phone _____

Policy Number _____

Coverage Amount _____

Beneficiaries _____

INDIVIDUAL RETIREMENT

List names of institutions and account numbers:

_____

_____

_____

MONEY MARKET AND MUTUAL FUNDS

Fund Names _____

Account Numbers _____

Phone _____

Location of Papers _____

CHARGE ACCOUNT AND CREDIT CARDS

Name of Card _____

Account Number _____

Phone _____

ANNUITIES

Company Name _____

Agent _____

Payable to/Beneficiary _____

Address _____

Phone _____

HEALTH INSURANCE

Company _____

Agent _____

Policy Number _____

Address _____

Phone _____

REAL ESTATE

Principle Address _____

Mortgage Holder _____

Address _____

Phone _____

Account Number _____

Pay Off Date _____

Property Insurance _____

Homeowners Insurance _____

Other Real Estate:

Location _____

Mortgage Holder _____

Account Number _____

Payoff _____

Renters:
Name _____
Address _____
Phone _____
Monthly Payment _____
Lease Duration _____

AUTOMOBILES
Make _____ Model _____ Year _____
Vehicle ID _____
Address _____
Phone _____
Account Number _____
Payoff Date _____

Auto Insurance
Company _____
Agent _____
Address _____
Phone _____
Policy Number _____

YOUR EXECUTIVE CABINET
Lawyer
TAX MAN
INSURANCE AGENT
BROKER
DOCTOR
CLERGY
GARDENER
PLUMBER
ELECRTICIAN

MEDICAL

TREATMENT DECISION CHECKLIST

Name _____   **Date** _____

Steps to completing a Living Will (directive to physician)

      1. Obtain form for your state.

      2. Consider any special instructions you wish to add.

      3. Sign in front of proper witnesses.

      4. Give copies (as appropriate) to:

  Names and date:

Steps to completing a durable Power of Attorney for health care

      1. Obtain form from your state.

      2. Select person to act as representative.

      3. Consider any special instructions you wish to add.

      4. Sign in front of proper witnesses.

      5. Give copies (as appropriate) to:

  Names and dates:

YOUR FUNERAL MASTER PLAN

Do you want a funeral or memorial service?

Do you want to be buried or cremated?

If you want to be cremated, have you already made arrangements with a cremation plan?

Do you want your ashes to be scattered?

Where?

How?

By whom?

If NOT SCATTERED,

If want my ashes placed:

If you want to be buried, do you want an open or closed casket?
Type of casket?
What funeral home do you want to use?
Have you made Pre need Arrangements with that director?
What cemetery?
Do you already have your plots?
Do you want graveside services?
Who do you want to perform your service?

Whom do you want for your pallbearers?
Usually 4-6
Whom do you want to do the readings for your service?

What Bible verses do you want used?
PSALMS
Old testament
Gospel
Do you want music?
A Soloist?
Which hymns do you wish to be sung?

Do you want flowers or money donated to a cause?
What cause?
What kind of flowers do you want for your casket?

What do you want to wear?
Do you want your rings, jewelry left on?
Hair, should your hair stylist be contacted
Other specific instruction
Do you want a reception or wake?

Where? Any ideas?

FURTHER INSTRUCTIONS:

SAMPLE CATHOLIC MASS
Church Choice
Choice of presiding Priest
Part 1 Introductory Rites
Pall? If yes, placed by priest, funeral home staff, friend or family
Do you want the placing of symbols?
Is there a specific bible you wish to be carried, by whom?
Cross? Is there a special cross? Designate by whom?
Choice of Opening Prayer
Part 11 Liturgy of the Word
Readings Old Testament, choice by whom
Responsorial psalm, choice, read by whom?
Alleluia verse
Gospel #
General intercession
Part 111 Liturgy of the Eucharist
Presentation of the gifts by whom?
Additional symbols, gifts, meaning, and whom to carry them?

Prayer after gifts#
Preface
Eucharistic prayer, after communion, prayer after communion

OUTLINE FOR WILL

I WANT TO GIVE TO MY;

FOR MY CHILDREN

If YOU HAVE MINOR CHILDREN

I HAVE MADE ARRANGEMENST FOR.......................... TO ACT AS LEGAL GARIAN FOR MY CHILDREN.

I HAVE MADE ARRANGEMENTS FOR...........................TO ACT AS THEIR TRUSTEE

I HAVE MADE THE ATTACHED FINANCIAL ARRANGMENTS FOR THEIR CONTINUED CARE

ABOUT MY CHILDREN

Medical information attached

Use this area to write in favorite foods, likes and dislikes, favorite toys, customs, anything that you feel would help your child's caregiver to better care for the child you love:

Instructions for child custody and care

PROVIDING FOR YOUR PET

Name of Pet _____

Age _____

Breed _____

Food/Medicines _____

Favorite Toys _____

Fears _____

Veterinarian _____

Medical records _____

Who will care for pet if I die _____

Special instructions _____

Financial provisions _____

Attach document for adoption of pet per pet

REQUEST FOR ADOPTION OF MY PET

I, _____, request that at the time of my death that my pet, _____, be adopted by _____.

My records of _____ care will be made available.

In consideration of your adoption of my beloved animal, I bequeath $_____ towards its future care.

_____   _____

Signature of owner   Date

I, _____, agree to accept the responsibility of adoption of pet, _____, and will do my best to give it loving care in your memory.

_____   _____

Signature of Adoptive Parent   Date

BIBLIOGRAPHY AND RESOURCES

PASSPORT TO A HAPPY DEATH RESOURCES

CATHOLIC FUNERAL
What Catholics Believe/Rev. Lawrence Lovarski, Radio Press
How To Handle Worry; A Catholic Approach/Marshall Cook/Pauline Books
The Cross and The Beatitudes/Fulton Sheen.Liquoria Press
Why Do Catholics Genuflect/Al Krestos Chars/Servant Publishing
Now is Eternity/Christopher Blumhadt, Plough Publishing
Catholic Etiquette-What You Need to Know about Catholic Rites and Wrongs/
Kay Lynn Huntington/Our Sunday Visitor Publishing Division
The Complete Idiots Guide to Understanding the Catechism/Bob Grma PhD/
Pearson Education Corp.
The Symbols of the Catholic Church/Maurice Dilasser/Liturgical Press
As I Lay Dying/Richard John Neuhaus/Basic Books
In Memoriam, Practical Guide to Planning A Memorial Service/Amanda Bennett/Terrence Foley/Fireside/Rockefeller Center
Order of Christian Funeral Catholic Book Publishing Co. NY 1989
Through Death to Life; Preparing to Celebrate the Funeral Mass, Rev. Joseph M.
Chaplin, Ave Maria Press, Notre Dame

FUNERALS
The Affordable Funeral, Going in Style, Not in Debt by R.R.E. Markin, Hooker
Press,
CR 96 Funeral Help program 1-800-0471

Consumer of Funeral Services Examining Boards
15 Northeast 3rd Street
P. O. Box 497
Washington, IN 47501
812-254-7887

Funeral and Memorial Societies of America
P. O. Box 10
Hinesburh, VT 05-461

Product Report: Preparing Your Own Funeral (D13188)
AARP Fulfillment (DEE 0139)
601 E Street NW
Washington, D.C. 20049

Federal Trade Commission, Funeral Rule
Attention: Public Records Branch
Room 130
Washington, D.C. 20580

IT'S YOUR CHOICE AARP BOOKS
Scott Foresman & Company
1865 Miner Street
Des Plaines, IL 6001
(Cost is $4.95 plus $1.75 postage, $3.00 if member plus postage)

Jewish Funeral Directors of America, Inc.
250 West 57th Street, Suite 2329
New York, NY 10107
212-582-8744

National Funeral directors and Mortician Association
1800 East Linwood Blvd.
Kansas city, MO 55346
816-921-1800

Pre-Arrangement Association of America
6321 Bury Drive, Suite 8
Eden Prairie, Minnesota 53346

F.H.P. (Funeral Help program, Division of Alzheimer's Research Foundation, Inc. of Virginia)
1236 Ginger Crescent

Virginia Beach, VA 23456
1-800-418-0471

RESOURCES ON DEATH
The American Way of Death/Jessica Mitford/Simon Schuster cr 1963
The Hour of Our Death/P. Aries/Vintage Books/1982
Ethical Issues in Death and Dying/T.L. Beauchamp/Prentice hall/1978
Psychological Care of the Dying Patient/C. Garfield/McGraw-Hill/1978

CHILDREN AND DEATH
When a Pet Dies/Fred Rogers/G.PO. Putnam's Sons/1988
The Grieving Child: A parent's Guide/Helen Fitzgerald/Fireside/1992
Talking About Death: A dialogue Between Parent and Child/Earl Grollman/
C.B. Slack/1992
Learning to Say Good-bye: when a parent Dies/Eda LeShan/MacMillan/1976
Lifetimes: The Beautiful Way to Explain Death to Children/Byran Mellonie and
Robert Ingpen/Bantam Books/1983

ORGAN DONATIONS

The Living Bank
P. O. Box 6725
Houston, TX 77265
713-528-2971

CREMATION
Cremation Association of North America
401 N. Michigan Avenue
Chicago, IL 60611
312-644-6610

RESOURCES
VETERANS

Burial at Sea
Retired Activities Section (Per-662c)
Bureau of Naval Personnel

Washington, D.C. 20370-6620
1-800-255-28950 or 1-703-614-3197

Office of Medical/Dental Affairs (Medden Affairs)
Mortuary Affairs, Bldg. 3811
Great Lakes, IL 60088-5200
1-800-376-1131, Ext. 629

Commandment (G-PMP-2)
U. S. Coast Guard
2100 Second Street, S.W.
Washington, D.C. 20593-0001
1-800-118-0471
1-800-722-1-202-267-2257/2259

Maritime Memorials International
P. O. Box 9106
Virginia Beach, VA 23450
1-800-118-0471

Burial in National Cemeteries
Superintendent
Arlington National Cemetery
Arlington, VA 22211-50
1-703-695-3250-3255

RESOURCES: DEALING WITH DEATH
The Human Encounter with Death/Grof and Halifax
Meditation and the Art of Dying/Pandit Usharbudh
Dialogue with Death/Eknath Easwaran
Counseling the Dying/Bower, Jackson, Knight, and LeShan
Until We Say Good-Bye/Elisabeth Kubler-Ross

RESOURCES: SUICIDE
Final Passages: Positive Choices for the Dying and Their Loved Ones/Dr. Jufotj
Ahromheim/New York: Simon & Schuster/1992
Last Wish/Betty Rolin/New York: Linden Press/Simon & Schuster/1985

Why People Kill Themselves: A 1980's Summary of Research on Suicidal Behavior/Springfield, IL/Charles C. Thomas/1983
Left Alive: After a Suicide in The Family/Linda Rosenfeld/New York; Fireside/Simon & Schuster/1984

Choice in Dying
200 Vartick Street, 10th Floor
New York, NY 10014-4810
212-366-5540

Compassion in Dying
P. O. Box 75295
Seattle, WA 98125
206-624-2775

Euthanasia Research and Guidance Organization
24829 Norris Lane
Junction City, OR 97448
503-998-1873

RESOURCES RELIGIOUS/SPIRITUAL
Crossing the Threshold of Hope, John Paul II/Edited by Vittorio Messori/Translated by Jenny McPhee and Martha McPhee/Alfred Knopf New York/1994
Life After Death/Tom Schouwiler San Diego/Greenhaven Press/1990
The Book of Angels: All Your Questions Answered/Carolyn Trickey Bapty/Baltimore: Oppenheimer Publishers/1994
Life After Life/Raymond Moody/Bantam Books/1976
The Afterlife: An Investigation into the Mysteries of Life and Life/Jenny Randles/Peter Hough/new York/Villard Books/1992

0-595-29452-9